Contents

// Example code in a Java Spring Security configuration @Override
protected void configure(HttpSecurity http) throws Exception {
http   .authorizeRequests()
.antMatchers("/admin/**").hasRole("ADMIN")

Chapter 1: Introduction to Visual Basic .NET (VB.NET)

1.1 What Is VB.NET?

Visual Basic .NET (VB.NET) is a versatile and powerful programming language that has gained popularity among developers for its simplicity and flexibility. It is part of the .NET framework, a comprehensive platform developed by Microsoft for building a wide range of applications, including desktop, web, mobile, and cloud-based applications. VB.NET is an evolution of the classic Visual Basic (VB) language, with enhancements that make it suitable for modern software development.

History of VB.NET

VB.NET has a rich history dating back to the original Visual Basic language, which was first released in 1991. Visual Basic became one of the most popular programming languages for Windows application development due to its user-friendly nature and rapid application development capabilities. However, as technology evolved, so did the demands on programming languages. This led to the development of VB.NET, which was introduced with the release of the .NET framework in the early 2000s.

VB.NET was designed to address the limitations of its predecessor and to leverage the power of the .NET framework. It brought several key improvements, including better support for object-oriented programming (OOP), a more modern and extensible architecture, and improved performance.

Advantages of VB.NET

VB.NET offers several advantages that make it an attractive choice for developers:

1. **Ease of Learning:** VB.NET has a straightforward and English-like syntax that is easy for beginners to grasp. It emphasizes readability and reduces the learning curve for new programmers.

2. **Rapid Application Development (RAD):** VB.NET provides a rich set of tools and controls for building Windows applications quickly. The drag-and-drop interface of the Visual Studio IDE (Integrated Development Environment) simplifies the creation of user interfaces.

3. **Strong Integration with Windows:** VB.NET is tightly integrated with the Windows operating system, making it an ideal choice for developing Windows desktop applications.

4. **Robust and Scalable:** VB.NET benefits from the .NET framework's robustness and scalability. Developers can build both small utilities and large enterprise-level applications with confidence.

5. **Large Developer Community:** VB.NET has a large and active developer community, which means access to resources, libraries, and support.

To start developing with VB.NET, you'll need the following:

- A computer running Windows with the Visual Studio IDE installed.
- Basic knowledge of programming concepts (though VB.NET is beginner-friendly).

Here's a simple "Hello, World!" program in VB.NET:

```
Module HelloWorld
    Sub Main()
        Console.WriteLine("Hello, World!")
    End Sub
End Module
```

In this example, we define a module named HelloWorld with a Main method that prints "Hello, World!" to the console. This is a basic introduction to the syntax of VB.NET.

As you progress through this book, you will delve deeper into the language and learn how to build a wide variety of applications, from desktop software to web applications and beyond. VB.NET's versatility and capabilities make it a valuable skill for any developer.

Stay tuned as we explore VB.NET in more detail in the subsequent chapters, covering fundamental concepts, advanced techniques, and real-world application development.

1.2 Historical Overview of VB.NET

To fully understand the significance of VB.NET, it's essential to explore its historical context. Visual Basic, the precursor to VB.NET, played a pivotal role in the world of software development. Here, we'll delve into the historical evolution of Visual Basic and how it paved the way for the development of VB.NET.

The Birth of Visual Basic

Visual Basic (VB) was first introduced by Microsoft in 1991. It emerged as a groundbreaking programming language because of its simplicity and ease of use. Unlike traditional languages that required extensive coding, VB offered a visual and intuitive development environment. Developers could create Windows applications by dragging and dropping graphical elements onto forms, which significantly accelerated application development.

VB quickly gained popularity among developers, both novice and experienced, due to its user-friendly nature. It enabled rapid application development (RAD) and became a staple for creating Windows-based software. VB's success led to various versions and updates, including Visual Basic 3, 4, 5, and 6.

The Limitations of Classic Visual Basic

While classic VB was beloved by many developers, it had its limitations. One of the primary drawbacks was its inability to easily work with the evolving technologies of the time, such as the internet and web-based applications. Additionally, classic VB was not well-suited for large-scale enterprise applications that required robustness, scalability, and maintainability.

As technology advanced, the demands on software development grew more complex. Developers needed a programming language that could seamlessly integrate with modern technologies and provide better support for object-oriented programming (OOP).

The Transition to VB.NET

The transition from classic VB to VB.NET was a significant turning point. VB.NET was introduced as part of the Microsoft .NET Framework in the early 2000s. It was a complete overhaul of the language, addressing many of the limitations of its predecessor.

Key Transformations:

1. **Object-Oriented Programming (OOP):** VB.NET embraced OOP principles, allowing developers to create more structured and modular code. This shift empowered developers to design applications with greater flexibility and maintainability.

2. **Interoperability:** VB.NET improved interoperability with other .NET languages, such as C#. This meant that developers could use components and libraries created in other languages seamlessly within their VB.NET projects.

3. **Web Development:** VB.NET was adapted for web development, making it suitable for building web applications and services using ASP.NET.

4. **Performance:** VB.NET brought significant performance improvements over classic VB, making it suitable for both desktop and enterprise-level applications.

5. **Modern Language Features:** It introduced modern language features, such as properties, events, and exception handling, aligning it with contemporary programming languages.

VB.NET's introduction marked a commitment to the .NET ecosystem and positioned Visual Basic as a language capable of meeting the demands of modern software development.

The Legacy of VB.NET

VB.NET's historical journey illustrates the adaptability and resilience of the Visual Basic language family. It has remained a popular choice for developers, particularly in scenarios where ease of use and rapid development are essential.

As we explore VB.NET in this book, we'll delve into its capabilities, features, and applications, equipping you with the knowledge and skills to harness the power of this versatile language. VB.NET continues to evolve, and its historical context provides valuable insights into its enduring relevance in the world of programming.

1.3 Advantages of VB.NET

Visual Basic .NET (VB.NET) offers a wide range of advantages that make it a compelling choice for software development. In this section, we'll explore some of the key benefits and strengths of VB.NET.

1. Beginner-Friendly Syntax

One of the standout features of VB.NET is its beginner-friendly syntax. The language is designed to be easy to learn and read, making it an excellent choice for those new to programming. VB.NET's syntax resembles plain English, with keywords and constructs that are intuitive. This simplicity reduces the learning curve, enabling newcomers to grasp programming concepts more easily.

Here's an example of a simple "Hello, World!" program in VB.NET:

```
Module HelloWorld
    Sub Main()
        Console.WriteLine("Hello, World!")
    End Sub
End Module
```

2. Rapid Application Development (RAD)

VB.NET excels in rapid application development (RAD). The Visual Studio IDE provides a rich set of tools and a visual designer that simplifies the creation of user interfaces. Developers can drag and drop controls onto forms, set properties, and write event handlers with ease. This RAD approach accelerates the development of Windows applications, making VB.NET an ideal choice for projects with tight deadlines.

3. Strong Integration with Windows

For desktop application development on the Windows platform, VB.NET offers seamless integration with the Windows operating system. Developers can access and leverage Windows features and libraries effortlessly. This integration allows for the creation of native Windows applications that provide a familiar user experience.

4. Robustness and Scalability

VB.NET inherits the robustness and scalability of the .NET framework. It is suitable for a wide range of application types, from small utilities to large-scale enterprise solutions. The .NET framework provides a robust foundation for building secure, high-performance applications. Additionally, VB.NET's support for object-oriented programming (OOP) enables developers to build modular and maintainable codebases, making it suitable for complex projects.

5. Large Developer Community

VB.NET boasts a large and active developer community. This community support is invaluable for developers seeking assistance, sharing knowledge, and accessing a wealth of resources, including libraries, frameworks, and extensions. The availability of community-contributed content enhances the development experience and ensures that help is readily available when needed.

6. Interoperability

VB.NET's interoperability is a significant advantage. It seamlessly integrates with other .NET languages like C#, allowing developers to leverage components and libraries written in different languages within the same project. This interoperability promotes code reuse and collaboration among developers with varying language preferences.

7. Modern Language Features

VB.NET introduced modern language features that align it with contemporary programming languages. These features include properties, events, exception handling, and support for advanced programming concepts like LINQ (Language-Integrated Query). These enhancements enable developers to write more efficient and expressive code.

8. Versatility

VB.NET's versatility is another key strength. While it is commonly associated with desktop application development, it is not limited to that domain. VB.NET can be used to develop web applications with ASP.NET, mobile apps with Xamarin, and even cloud-enabled applications. This versatility allows developers to adapt to different project requirements and explore various domains of software development.

In conclusion, VB.NET's advantages, including its beginner-friendly syntax, rapid development capabilities, integration with Windows, robustness, and interoperability, make it a valuable choice for developers. Whether you're a newcomer to programming or an experienced developer, VB.NET provides a versatile and powerful platform for building a wide range of applications.

1.4 Getting Started with VB.NET

Now that we've explored the advantages and historical context of VB.NET, let's dive into the practical steps to get started with VB.NET development. This section will guide you through the essential tools, setup, and basic concepts you need to begin your journey with VB.NET.

1.4.1 Setting Up Your Development Environment

Before you start coding in VB.NET, you need to set up your development environment. Here are the key components you'll need:

1. Visual Studio IDE

Microsoft Visual Studio is the primary integrated development environment for VB.NET. It provides a feature-rich environment for writing, debugging, and testing your VB.NET applications. You can download Visual Studio from the official Microsoft website. There are different editions available, including a free Community edition that is suitable for individual developers and small teams.

2. .NET Framework

VB.NET is part of the .NET framework, so you'll need to ensure that you have the .NET framework installed on your computer. Visual Studio typically includes the necessary framework components, so you may not need to install it separately.

3. Creating a New VB.NET Project

Once you have Visual Studio installed and ready, you can create a new VB.NET project. Follow these steps:

1. Launch Visual Studio.
2. Click on "File" in the menu bar.
3. Select "New" and then "Project..."
4. In the "Create a new project" window, choose "Visual Basic" under "Project Types."
5. Select a project template based on your application type (e.g., Windows Forms App, Console App, ASP.NET Web App).
6. Provide a name and location for your project.
7. Click "Create."

Visual Studio will create a new VB.NET project for you, complete with a starter code template based on the chosen project type.

4. Writing and Running Your First VB.NET Program

Let's write a simple "Hello, World!" program to get started. In a Windows Forms Application project, you can use the code below:

```
Public Class MainForm
    Private Sub btnSayHello_Click(sender As Object, e As EventArgs) Handles b
tnSayHello.Click
        MessageBox.Show("Hello, World!", "VB.NET")
    End Sub
End Class
```

In this example, we create a Windows Forms application with a button (btnSayHello) and an event handler that displays a message box when the button is clicked.

Visual Studio provides powerful debugging tools that help you identify and fix issues in your code. You can set breakpoints, inspect variables, and step through your code to understand its execution flow.

To test your application, simply click the "Start Debugging" button (usually a green arrow) in Visual Studio. This will compile and run your VB.NET program, allowing you to interact with it and observe its behavior.

With these steps, you've set up your VB.NET development environment and created and run your first VB.NET program. As you continue your journey with VB.NET, you'll explore more advanced topics and build increasingly complex applications. The combination of the user-friendly VB.NET language and the powerful Visual Studio IDE provides a solid foundation for your development endeavors.

1.5 Setting Up Your Development Environment

Setting up your development environment for VB.NET is a crucial step in your journey as a VB.NET developer. In this section, we'll delve into the details of configuring your development environment to ensure that you have everything you need to write, debug, and test your VB.NET applications effectively.

1.5.1 Installing Visual Studio

Microsoft Visual Studio is the go-to integrated development environment (IDE) for VB.NET development. To get started, you'll need to install Visual Studio:

1. Visit the official Microsoft Visual Studio download page.
2. Download the Visual Studio installer for your desired edition. There is a free Community edition available, which is suitable for most developers.
3. Run the installer and follow the on-screen instructions.

During installation, you can customize your installation by selecting the components you need. Ensure that you include the ".NET desktop development" workload, as it contains tools and libraries essential for VB.NET development.

1.5.2 .NET Framework

VB.NET relies on the .NET Framework, which provides a runtime environment and libraries for running VB.NET applications. Fortunately, Visual Studio typically includes the necessary .NET Framework components, so you may not need to install it separately.

1.5.3 Creating a VB.NET Project

With Visual Studio installed, you can create your first VB.NET project:

1. Launch Visual Studio.

2. Click on "File" in the menu bar.
3. Select "New" and then "Project…"
4. In the "Create a new project" window, choose "Visual Basic" under "Project Types."
5. Select a project template based on your application type (e.g., Windows Forms App, Console App, ASP.NET Web App).
6. Provide a name and location for your project.
7. Click "Create."

Visual Studio will generate a new VB.NET project with a starter code template tailored to your chosen project type.

1.5.4 Writing VB.NET Code

You can start writing VB.NET code in Visual Studio immediately. For example, in a Windows Forms Application project, you can create a simple "Hello, World!" program:

```
Public Class MainForm
    Private Sub btnSayHello_Click(sender As Object, e As EventArgs) Handles b
tnSayHello.Click
        MessageBox.Show("Hello, World!", "VB.NET")
    End Sub
End Class
```

In this code, we define a Windows Forms application with a button (btnSayHello) and an event handler that displays a message box when the button is clicked.

1.5.5 Debugging and Testing

Visual Studio offers robust debugging tools that assist you in identifying and resolving issues in your VB.NET code. You can set breakpoints, inspect variables, and step through your code to understand its execution flow.

To test your VB.NET application, click the "Start Debugging" button (usually a green arrow) in Visual Studio. This will compile and run your application, allowing you to interact with it and observe its behavior.

1.5.6 Extensions and Add-ons

Visual Studio can be further enhanced with extensions and add-ons that provide additional functionality and tools for specific tasks. Explore the Visual Studio Marketplace to discover extensions that suit your development needs, such as code analysis tools, code generators, and source control integrations.

By following these steps and customizing your development environment to your preferences, you'll be well-equipped to embark on your VB.NET development journey. Visual Studio's robust features and the .NET framework's support for VB.NET make it a powerful platform for building a wide range of applications.

Chapter 2: VB.NET Fundamentals

2.1 Data Types and Variables

In VB.NET, as in any programming language, data types and variables play a fundamental role. Understanding data types and how to work with variables is essential for writing effective code. In this section, we'll explore the concept of data types, learn about some commonly used data types in VB.NET, and discover how to declare and use variables.

2.1.1 What Are Data Types?

Data types define the type of data that a variable can hold. They specify the range of values that a variable can store and the operations that can be performed on it. VB.NET is a strongly typed language, which means that every variable and expression has a specific data type associated with it.

Here are some of the commonly used data types in VB.NET:

- **Integer (Integer):** Used for storing whole numbers, both positive and negative.
- **Double (Double):** Used for storing floating-point numbers with decimal places.
- **String (String):** Used for storing text data.
- **Boolean (Boolean):** Used for representing true or false values.
- **Date (Date):** Used for storing date and time values.
- **Char (Char):** Used for storing single characters.

2.1.2 Declaring Variables

In VB.NET, you declare a variable before using it. To declare a variable, you specify its data type followed by its name. Here's a basic example:

```
Dim age As Integer
```

In this example, we declare a variable named `age` with the data type `Integer`. This variable can store whole numbers.

You can also declare and initialize a variable in a single line:

```
Dim name As String = "John"
```

Here, we declare a `String` variable named `name` and assign it the initial value "John."

2.1.3 Variable Naming Rules

When naming variables in VB.NET, there are some rules to follow:

- Variable names must begin with a letter or an underscore (_).
- They can contain letters, numbers, and underscores.

- Variable names are case-insensitive, but it's a good practice to use meaningful and consistent casing for readability.
- Reserved words, such as keywords (e.g., `Dim`, `If`, `While`), cannot be used as variable names.

2.1.4 Assigning Values to Variables

You can assign values to variables using the assignment operator (`=`). For example:

```
age = 30
```

This assigns the value 30 to the `age` variable.

2.1.5 Working with Data Types

VB.NET provides various functions and methods to work with data types. For example, you can convert data from one type to another using type conversion functions like `CInt()`, `CDbl()`, and `CStr()`. Here's an example of type conversion:

```
Dim numString As String = "42"
Dim num As Integer = CInt(numString)
```

In this example, we convert the string "42" to an integer using the `CInt()` function.

2.1.6 Constants

In addition to variables, you can define constants in VB.NET using the `Const` keyword. Constants are values that do not change during the execution of a program. They are often used for defining values that should remain constant throughout the program's lifetime.

```
Const PI As Double = 3.14159
```

Here, we define a constant named `PI` with a value of 3.14159.

Understanding data types and variables is foundational for programming in VB.NET. They enable you to store, manipulate, and work with different types of data in your applications. As you progress in your VB.NET journey, you'll discover more complex data types and learn how to use them effectively in your programs.

2.2 Operators and Expressions

Operators and expressions are fundamental components of VB.NET that allow you to perform various calculations, comparisons, and operations on data. In this section, we'll explore the different types of operators in VB.NET and how to construct expressions using these operators.

2.2.1 Arithmetic Operators

Arithmetic operators are used for performing mathematical calculations. Here are some common arithmetic operators in VB.NET:

- **Addition (+):** Adds two numbers.
- **Subtraction (-):** Subtracts the right operand from the left operand.
- **Multiplication (*):** Multiplies two numbers.
- **Division (/):** Divides the left operand by the right operand.
- **Modulus (Mod):** Returns the remainder of the division of the left operand by the right operand.
- **Exponentiation (^):** Raises the left operand to the power of the right operand.

Here's an example of using arithmetic operators:

```
Dim a As Integer = 10
Dim b As Integer = 5

Dim sum As Integer = a + b ' sum = 15
Dim difference As Integer = a - b ' difference = 5
Dim product As Integer = a * b ' product = 50
Dim quotient As Integer = a / b ' quotient = 2
Dim remainder As Integer = a Mod b ' remainder = 0
Dim power As Integer = a ^ b ' power = 100000
```

2.2.2 Comparison Operators

Comparison operators are used to compare two values or expressions. They return a Boolean result (True or False) based on the comparison. Here are some common comparison operators in VB.NET:

- **Equal To (=):** Checks if two values are equal.
- **Not Equal To (<>):** Checks if two values are not equal.
- **Greater Than (>):** Checks if the left operand is greater than the right operand.
- **Less Than (<):** Checks if the left operand is less than the right operand.
- **Greater Than or Equal To (>=):** Checks if the left operand is greater than or equal to the right operand.
- **Less Than or Equal To (<=):** Checks if the left operand is less than or equal to the right operand.

Here's an example of using comparison operators:

```
Dim x As Integer = 10
Dim y As Integer = 20

Dim isEqual As Boolean = (x = y) ' isEqual = False
Dim isNotEqual As Boolean = (x <> y) ' isNotEqual = True
Dim isGreater As Boolean = (x > y) ' isGreater = False
Dim isLess As Boolean = (x < y) ' isLess = True
```

```
Dim isGreaterOrEqual As Boolean = (x >= y) ' isGreaterOrEqual = False
Dim isLessOrEqual As Boolean = (x <= y) ' isLessOrEqual = True
```

2.2.3 Logical Operators

Logical operators are used to perform logical operations on Boolean values. They are often used in conditional statements and expressions. Here are the logical operators in VB.NET:

- **And:** Returns True if both operands are True.
- **Or:** Returns True if at least one of the operands is True.
- **Not:** Returns the opposite Boolean value of the operand.

Here's an example of using logical operators:

```
Dim p As Boolean = True
Dim q As Boolean = False

Dim andResult As Boolean = (p And q) ' andResult = False
Dim orResult As Boolean = (p Or q) ' orResult = True
Dim notResult As Boolean = Not p ' notResult = False
```

2.2.4 Concatenation Operator

In addition to mathematical and logical operators, VB.NET also provides a concatenation operator (&) for joining strings together. This operator is used to concatenate or combine strings into a single string.

```
Dim firstName As String = "John"
Dim lastName As String = "Doe"

Dim fullName As String = firstName & " " & lastName ' fullName = "John Doe"
```

Operators and expressions are essential for performing various operations and making decisions in your VB.NET programs. As you continue to explore VB.NET, you'll encounter more operators and learn how to use them effectively to manipulate data and control the flow of your applications.

2.3 Control Structures (If Statements, Loops)

Control structures are essential elements of programming that allow you to control the flow of your code. In VB.NET, you can use control structures to make decisions (conditional statements) and repeat a block of code (loops). Let's explore two fundamental control structures: If statements and loops.

2.3.1 If Statements

If statements, also known as conditional statements, allow you to execute specific code blocks based on a condition. In VB.NET, the basic structure of an If statement is as follows:

```vbnet
If condition Then
    ' Code to execute if the condition is True
End If
```

Here's an example:

```vbnet
Dim age As Integer = 25

If age >= 18 Then
    Console.WriteLine("You are an adult.")
End If
```

In this example, the code inside the If block is executed because the condition age >= 18 is True.

If-Else Statements

You can extend If statements with an Else block to provide an alternative code path for when the condition is False:

```vbnet
If condition Then
    ' Code to execute if the condition is True
Else
    ' Code to execute if the condition is False
End If
```

Here's an example:

```vbnet
Dim grade As Integer = 65

If grade >= 70 Then
    Console.WriteLine("Passing grade.")
Else
    Console.WriteLine("Failing grade.")
End If
```

If-ElseIf Statements

For handling multiple conditions, you can use ElseIf clauses:

```vbnet
If condition1 Then
    ' Code to execute if condition1 is True
ElseIf condition2 Then
    ' Code to execute if condition2 is True
Else
    ' Code to execute if all conditions are False
End If
```

2.3.2 Loops

Loops allow you to repeat a block of code multiple times. VB.NET provides several types of loops, including For, While, and Do While loops.

For Loop

The For loop is commonly used when you know how many times you want to repeat a block of code. Here's an example:

```
For i As Integer = 1 To 5
    Console.WriteLine("Iteration " & i)
Next
```

In this example, the code inside the For loop is executed five times, as specified by the loop range 1 To 5.

While Loop

The While loop is used when you want to repeat a block of code while a condition is True:

```
Dim count As Integer = 1

While count <= 5
    Console.WriteLine("Count: " & count)
    count += 1
End While
```

This loop continues as long as the count variable is less than or equal to 5.

Do While Loop

The Do While loop is similar to the While loop but evaluates the condition at the end of the loop:

```
Dim number As Integer = 1

Do While number <= 5
    Console.WriteLine("Number: " & number)
    number += 1
Loop
```

The code inside the loop is executed at least once before checking the condition.

Exiting Loops

You can exit a loop prematurely using the Exit statement. For example, you can exit a loop when a certain condition is met:

```
For i As Integer = 1 To 10
    If i = 5 Then
        Exit For
    End If
    Console.WriteLine("Iteration " & i)
Next
```

2.3.3 Nested Control Structures

Control structures can be nested within each other to create more complex behavior. For example, you can have an If statement inside a For loop or vice versa to control program flow based on multiple conditions.

```
For i As Integer = 1 To 5
    If i Mod 2 = 0 Then
        Console.WriteLine(i & " is even.")
    Else
        Console.WriteLine(i & " is odd.")
    End If
Next
```

This code uses a For loop to iterate through numbers from 1 to 5 and an If statement to determine whether each number is even or odd.

Control structures are essential for creating dynamic and decision-driven programs. By combining If statements and loops, you can control the flow of your code and perform various tasks, from making decisions based on conditions to iterating through collections of data. These fundamental concepts are the building blocks of more complex VB.NET applications.

2.4 Functions and Procedures

Functions and procedures are essential components of VB.NET that allow you to organize and reuse code. They enable you to break down your code into smaller, manageable units, making it more modular and maintainable. In this section, we'll explore the concepts of functions and procedures in VB.NET.

2.4.1 Functions

A function is a block of code that performs a specific task and returns a value. Functions are defined with a name, a list of parameters (optional), and a return type. The return type specifies the type of value that the function will return when it completes its task. Here's a basic function definition in VB.NET:

```
Function AddNumbers(ByVal num1 As Integer, ByVal num2 As Integer) As Integer
    Dim result As Integer = num1 + num2
    Return result
End Function
```

In this example, we define a function named AddNumbers that takes two integer parameters (num1 and num2) and returns an integer. The function calculates the sum of num1 and num2 and returns the result using the Return statement.

You can call this function as follows:

```
Dim sum As Integer = AddNumbers(5, 7)
Console.WriteLine("Sum: " & sum) ' Output: Sum: 12
```

Functions are reusable pieces of code that can be called from various parts of your program. They help promote code reusability and maintainability.

Procedures, also known as subroutines, are similar to functions but do not return a value. They perform a specific task or a sequence of actions but do not produce a result. Procedure definitions look similar to function definitions, but they use the Sub keyword instead of Function:

```
Sub DisplayMessage(ByVal message As String)
    Console.WriteLine(message)
End Sub
```

In this example, we define a procedure named DisplayMessage that takes a single string parameter (message) and displays it to the console.

You can call this procedure as follows:

```
DisplayMessage("Hello, VB.NET!") ' Output: Hello, VB.NET!
```

Procedures are useful for organizing code that needs to perform actions but does not need to return values. They help improve code readability and maintainability by encapsulating specific functionality.

Both functions and procedures can accept parameters, which are values or variables that you pass to them when calling. Parameters allow you to customize the behavior of functions and procedures by providing input data.

There are two types of parameters in VB.NET:

- **Value Parameters (ByVal):** Value parameters pass a copy of the actual value or variable to the function or procedure. Any changes made to the parameter inside the function or procedure do not affect the original value or variable.

- **Reference Parameters (ByRef):** Reference parameters pass a reference to the actual value or variable to the function or procedure. Changes made to the parameter inside the function or procedure affect the original value or variable.

Here's an example of using both types of parameters:

```
Sub ModifyValue(ByVal x As Integer, ByRef y As Integer)
    x = x + 10
    y = y + 10
End Sub
```

```
Dim a As Integer = 5
Dim b As Integer = 5

ModifyValue(a, b)

Console.WriteLine("a: " & a) ' Output: a: 5
Console.WriteLine("b: " & b) ' Output: b: 15
```

In this example, the ModifyValue procedure takes a value parameter x and a reference parameter y. Changes made to x do not affect the original value of a, but changes to y affect the original value of b.

Functions and procedures, along with parameters, are essential tools for building structured and modular code in VB.NET. They allow you to create reusable components and improve code organization, making your programs more efficient and maintainable.

2.5 Debugging and Error Handling

Debugging and error handling are critical aspects of software development in VB.NET. Debugging helps you identify and fix issues in your code, while error handling allows you to gracefully manage and recover from unexpected errors or exceptions. In this section, we'll explore the tools and techniques available for debugging and error handling in VB.NET.

2.5.1 Debugging Tools

VB.NET provides a range of debugging tools to help you pinpoint and resolve issues in your code. Some of the key debugging tools and techniques include:

Breakpoints

Breakpoints allow you to pause the execution of your program at a specific line of code. You can set breakpoints by clicking in the left margin of the code editor or by pressing F9. When the program reaches a breakpoint, it enters debug mode, allowing you to inspect variables and step through code.

Debugging Windows

Visual Studio offers various debugging windows, such as the Locals window, Watch window, and Immediate window. These windows allow you to view variable values, evaluate expressions, and interactively explore your code during debugging.

Stepping Through Code

You can step through your code using debugging commands like Step Into (F11), Step Over (F10), and Step Out (Shift+F11). These commands help you navigate through your code one line at a time and understand its execution flow.

During debugging, exceptions are highlighted, and you can configure Visual Studio to break on specific exceptions, making it easier to identify and resolve issues in your code.

Debugging Symbols

Debugging symbols (PDB files) generated during compilation contain information about your code's structure and variable names. They are essential for debugging, as they enable Visual Studio to map machine code to your source code.

2.5.2 Handling Exceptions

Exception handling allows you to gracefully handle errors that may occur during program execution. Exceptions are unexpected events or conditions that can disrupt the normal flow of your code. VB.NET provides a structured way to handle exceptions using Try-Catch blocks:

```
Try
    ' Code that may cause an exception
    Dim result As Integer = 10 / 0 ' This will raise a DivideByZeroException
Catch ex As Exception
    ' Handle the exception
    Console.WriteLine("An exception occurred: " & ex.Message)
End Try
```

In this example, the code inside the Try block attempts to perform a division by zero, which would raise a `DivideByZeroException`. The Catch block captures the exception and allows you to handle it gracefully.

Catching Specific Exceptions

You can catch specific exceptions by specifying their types in Catch blocks. This allows you to handle different types of exceptions differently:

```
Try
    Dim result As Integer = 10 / 0
Catch ex As DivideByZeroException
    Console.WriteLine("Division by zero error: " & ex.Message)
Catch ex As Exception
    Console.WriteLine("An unexpected error occurred: " & ex.Message)
End Try
```

In this example, we catch a `DivideByZeroException` specifically and handle it differently from other types of exceptions.

Finally Block

You can also use a Finally block to specify code that must be executed regardless of whether an exception occurred. This is useful for cleanup operations:

```vbnet
Try
    ' Code that may cause an exception
Catch ex As Exception
    ' Handle the exception
Finally
    ' Cleanup code (will always execute)
End Try
```

2.5.3 Logging and Error Reporting

Logging is an essential practice for monitoring and diagnosing issues in production applications. You can use logging frameworks like log4net or built-in logging libraries to record information about errors and program behavior. This allows you to review logs and identify the root causes of issues.

Error reporting mechanisms, such as email notifications or integration with error tracking services, can alert you to critical errors in your application when they occur in production. This proactive approach helps you address issues quickly and improve the reliability of your software.

Debugging and error handling are crucial skills for VB.NET developers. By effectively using debugging tools, handling exceptions, and implementing logging and error reporting, you can ensure that your VB.NET applications are robust, reliable, and maintainable, even in the face of unexpected issues.

Chapter 3: Object-Oriented Programming (OOP) in VB.NET

3.1 Understanding Objects and Classes

Object-Oriented Programming (OOP) is a programming paradigm that focuses on organizing code into objects, which are instances of classes. In VB.NET, as in many modern programming languages, OOP plays a central role in structuring and designing applications. In this section, we'll delve into the fundamental concepts of objects and classes in VB.NET.

3.1.1 What Are Objects and Classes?

- **Class:** A class is a blueprint or a template for creating objects. It defines the structure and behavior that objects of the class will have. In VB.NET, classes are used to model real-world entities, concepts, or abstract data types. For example, you can have a Person class to represent individuals or a Car class to represent vehicles.

- **Object:** An object is an instance of a class. It is a concrete realization of the class's blueprint, with its own unique data and state. Objects encapsulate data (attributes or properties) and behavior (methods or functions) related to the class. For instance, you can create an object of the Person class to represent a specific person, such as "John Doe."

3.1.2 Key Concepts of OOP

Encapsulation

Encapsulation is one of the core principles of OOP. It refers to the bundling of data (attributes or properties) and methods (functions) that operate on that data into a single unit, i.e., the class. This unit is called an object. Encapsulation allows you to hide the internal details of how an object works, exposing only the necessary interfaces to interact with it. This promotes data privacy and prevents unintended modification of an object's state.

Inheritance

Inheritance allows you to create a new class (the derived or child class) based on an existing class (the base or parent class). The derived class inherits the attributes and methods of the base class and can also have additional attributes and methods of its own. Inheritance promotes code reuse and the creation of a hierarchy of related classes.

Polymorphism

Polymorphism means "many shapes." It allows objects of different classes to be treated as objects of a common base class. This enables you to write code that can work with objects of multiple classes without needing to know their specific types. Polymorphism is often achieved through method overriding, where a derived class provides its implementation of a method defined in the base class.

Abstraction is the process of simplifying complex systems by breaking them into smaller, more manageable parts. In OOP, classes and objects provide a form of abstraction. A class abstracts the properties and behaviors of real-world entities, allowing you to model and work with complex systems in a structured way.

3.1.3 Declaring Classes

In VB.NET, you declare a class using the `Class` keyword, followed by the class name. Here's a simple example of declaring a `Person` class:

```
Public Class Person
    ' Fields (attributes)
    Public Name As String
    Public Age As Integer

    ' Methods (functions)
    Public Sub SayHello()
        Console.WriteLine("Hello, my name is " & Name & " and I am " & Age &
" years old.")
    End Sub
End Class
```

In this example, the `Person` class has two fields (attributes): `Name` and `Age`, and one method: `SayHello`.

3.1.4 Creating Objects

To create an object (an instance) of a class, you use the `New` keyword followed by the class name. Here's how you create a `Person` object:

```
Dim john As New Person()
john.Name = "John Doe"
john.Age = 30
john.SayHello() ' Output: Hello, my name is John Doe and I am 30 years old.
```

In this code, we create a `Person` object named `john` and set its `Name` and `Age` properties. Then, we call the `SayHello` method to introduce John.

Understanding objects and classes is fundamental to OOP in VB.NET. It provides a structured way to model and organize code, making it more modular and easier to maintain. As you continue to explore OOP, you'll dive deeper into concepts like inheritance, polymorphism, and encapsulation, which enable you to build complex and flexible software systems.

3.2 Inheritance and Polymorphism

Inheritance and polymorphism are key concepts in object-oriented programming (OOP) that allow you to create more organized and efficient code by reusing and extending existing classes. In this section, we'll explore inheritance and polymorphism in the context of VB.NET.

3.2.1 Inheritance

Inheritance is a mechanism in OOP that allows you to create a new class (the derived or child class) based on an existing class (the base or parent class). The derived class inherits the attributes (fields or properties) and methods (functions) of the base class, and it can also have additional attributes and methods of its own.

In VB.NET, you use the `Inherits` keyword to declare inheritance. Here's an example:

```
Public Class Animal
    Public Sub Eat()
        Console.WriteLine("The animal is eating.")
    End Sub
End Class

Public Class Dog
    Inherits Animal

    Public Sub Bark()
        Console.WriteLine("The dog is barking.")
    End Sub
End Class
```

In this example, we have a base class `Animal` with an `Eat` method, and a derived class `Dog` that inherits from `Animal`. The `Dog` class also has its own method `Bark`. This allows a `Dog` object to both eat (inherited from `Animal`) and bark.

3.2.2 Polymorphism

Polymorphism, which means "many shapes," allows objects of different classes to be treated as objects of a common base class. It enables you to write code that can work with objects of multiple classes without needing to know their specific types.

Polymorphism is often achieved through method overriding, where a derived class provides its implementation of a method defined in the base class. In VB.NET, you use the `Overrides` keyword to indicate method overriding. Here's an example:

```
Public Class Shape
    Public Overridable Sub Draw()
        Console.WriteLine("Drawing a shape.")
    End Sub
```

```vbnet
End Class

Public Class Circle
    Inherits Shape

    Public Overrides Sub Draw()
        Console.WriteLine("Drawing a circle.")
    End Sub
End Class

Public Class Rectangle
    Inherits Shape

    Public Overrides Sub Draw()
        Console.WriteLine("Drawing a rectangle.")
    End Sub
End Class
```

In this example, we have a base class Shape with a Draw method marked as Overridable. Two derived classes, Circle and Rectangle, override the Draw method to provide their implementations.

Using polymorphism, you can work with objects of these classes through a common base class:

```vbnet
Dim shapes As New List(Of Shape)
shapes.Add(New Circle())
shapes.Add(New Rectangle())

For Each shape As Shape In shapes
    shape.Draw()
Next
```

The output of this code will be:

```
Drawing a circle.
Drawing a rectangle.
```

Even though the objects in the shapes list are of different derived classes (Circle and Rectangle), polymorphism allows us to call the Draw method on each of them without knowing their specific types.

Inheritance and polymorphism are powerful concepts in OOP that promote code reuse, modularity, and flexibility. By organizing your classes in a hierarchical manner and using method overriding, you can create more maintainable and extensible code in VB.NET. These principles are fundamental in building complex software systems.

3.3 Encapsulation and Abstraction

Encapsulation and abstraction are fundamental principles of object-oriented programming (OOP) that help you create more maintainable and modular code. In this section, we'll explore these concepts in the context of VB.NET.

3.3.1 Encapsulation

Encapsulation is one of the core principles of OOP, and it refers to the bundling of data (attributes or properties) and methods (functions) that operate on that data into a single unit, which is the class. Encapsulation allows you to hide the internal details of how an object works, exposing only the necessary interfaces to interact with it. This promotes data privacy and prevents unintended modification of an object's state.

In VB.NET, you can implement encapsulation by defining class members (fields or properties) with appropriate access modifiers such as `Private`, `Protected`, `Public`, or `Friend`. These modifiers control the visibility of class members from outside the class.

Here's an example of encapsulation:

```
Public Class BankAccount
    Private balance As Decimal

    Public Sub Deposit(amount As Decimal)
        If amount > 0 Then
            balance += amount
        End If
    End Sub

    Public Sub Withdraw(amount As Decimal)
        If amount > 0 AndAlso amount <= balance Then
            balance -= amount
        End If
    End Sub

    Public Function GetBalance() As Decimal
        Return balance
    End Function
End Class
```

In this `BankAccount` class, the `balance` field is declared as `Private`, making it inaccessible from outside the class. The `Deposit`, `Withdraw`, and `GetBalance` methods provide controlled access to the `balance` field, allowing clients to interact with the bank account while encapsulating the internal state.

3.3.2 Abstraction

Abstraction is the process of simplifying complex systems by breaking them into smaller, more manageable parts. In OOP, classes and objects provide a form of abstraction. A class abstracts the properties and behaviors of real-world entities, allowing you to model and work with complex systems in a structured way.

Abstraction helps in managing complexity by focusing on essential details while hiding unnecessary complexity. For example, when working with a Car object, you may not need to know the intricate details of how the engine works. Instead, you can abstract the engine's behavior using methods like Start and Stop.

Here's an example of abstraction:

```
Public Class Car
    Private engineRunning As Boolean = False

    Public Sub Start()
        engineRunning = True
        Console.WriteLine("Car engine started.")
    End Sub

    Public Sub StopEngine()
        engineRunning = False
        Console.WriteLine("Car engine stopped.")
    End Sub
End Class
```

In this Car class, we abstract the behavior of the car's engine by providing methods to start and stop it. The client code interacts with the Car class through these abstracted methods, simplifying the usage of the object.

Abstraction allows you to focus on the essential aspects of an object and its interactions, leading to more maintainable and comprehensible code. It also enables you to work at higher levels of abstraction when designing and implementing complex software systems.

Encapsulation and abstraction are key building blocks of OOP in VB.NET. By encapsulating data and controlling access to it and abstracting complex behavior, you can create classes that are more manageable, reusable, and adaptable to changes in your software requirements. These principles promote code organization and maintainability, making your codebase more robust and easier to maintain.

3.4 Interfaces and Abstract Classes

Interfaces and abstract classes are advanced object-oriented programming (OOP) concepts in VB.NET that facilitate the development of flexible and extensible software systems. In this section, we'll explore interfaces and abstract classes and their role in designing software.

3.4.1 Interfaces

An interface defines a contract that a class must adhere to. It specifies a set of method signatures (functions) and properties (variables) that a class implementing the interface must provide. Interfaces allow you to define a common set of behaviors that multiple classes can share, promoting code reusability and flexibility.

Here's an example of an interface called IDrawable:

```
Public Interface IDrawable
    Sub Draw()
    Property Color As String
End Interface
```

In this interface, there are two members: a Sub method named Draw and a Property named Color. Any class that implements the IDrawable interface must provide implementations for these members.

Let's create a class that implements the IDrawable interface:

```
Public Class Circle
    Implements IDrawable

    Public Property Color As String Implements IDrawable.Color

    Public Sub Draw() Implements IDrawable.Draw
        Console.WriteLine($"Drawing a {Color} circle.")
    End Sub
End Class
```

In this example, the Circle class implements the IDrawable interface, providing its implementation for the Draw method and the Color property. This allows instances of the Circle class to be treated as IDrawable objects.

3.4.2 Abstract Classes

An abstract class is a class that cannot be instantiated on its own but serves as a base for other classes. Abstract classes can define both concrete methods (with implementations) and abstract methods (without implementations). Subclasses that inherit from an abstract class must provide implementations for its abstract methods.

Here's an example of an abstract class named Shape:

```
Public MustInherit Class Shape
    Public MustOverride Sub Draw()

    Public Sub Move(x As Integer, y As Integer)
        Console.WriteLine($"Moving the shape to ({x}, {y}).")
```

```
      End Sub
End Class
```

In this abstract class, we have an abstract method `Draw` and a concrete method `Move`. Any class that inherits from `Shape` must implement the `Draw` method.

Let's create a concrete class that inherits from `Shape`:

```
Public Class Circle
    Inherits Shape

    Public Overrides Sub Draw()
        Console.WriteLine("Drawing a circle.")
    End Sub
End Class
```

In this example, the `Circle` class inherits from `Shape` and provides its implementation for the `Draw` method. It is required to do so because `Draw` is an abstract method in the base `Shape` class.

3.4.3 When to Use Interfaces and Abstract Classes

Interfaces are suitable when you want to define a contract for multiple classes that may not share a common base class. They allow classes with different inheritance hierarchies to implement common behaviors.

Abstract classes are useful when you want to provide a common base for a group of related classes and enforce a certain structure or behavior. They can contain both abstract and concrete members, providing a balance between consistency and flexibility.

In summary, interfaces and abstract classes are essential tools for designing extensible and maintainable software in VB.NET. They enable you to define common behaviors and structures that can be shared among multiple classes, promoting code reusability and maintainability. Choosing between interfaces and abstract classes depends on your specific design requirements and goals.

3.5 Working with Objects in VB.NET

Working with objects is at the core of object-oriented programming (OOP), and VB.NET provides powerful features and tools for creating, manipulating, and interacting with objects. In this section, we'll explore various aspects of working with objects in VB.NET.

3.5.1 Creating Objects

In VB.NET, you create objects by instantiating classes. To create an object, you use the `New` keyword followed by the class name, like this:

```
Dim myObject As New MyClass()
```

This statement creates a new instance of the MyClass class and assigns it to the myObject variable. You can then use this object to access its properties and methods.

3.5.2 Accessing Properties and Methods

Once you have an object, you can access its properties and methods using the dot notation. For example, if the MyClass class has a property called Name and a method called PrintName, you can access them like this:

```
myObject.Name = "John"
myObject.PrintName() ' Calls the PrintName method of myObject
```

3.5.3 Object Initialization

VB.NET allows you to initialize object properties during object creation using constructors. A constructor is a special method in a class that is called when an object is created. You can define your constructors to accept parameters and initialize object properties based on those parameters.

Here's an example of a class with a constructor:

```
Public Class Person
    Public Property Name As String

    ' Constructor that accepts a name parameter
    Public Sub New(name As String)
        Me.Name = name
    End Sub
End Class
```

You can create a Person object and initialize its Name property like this:

```
Dim john As New Person("John")
Console.WriteLine(john.Name) ' Output: John
```

3.5.4 Object Comparison

In VB.NET, you can compare objects using the Is operator to check if two references point to the same object in memory. For example:

```
Dim obj1 As New MyClass()
Dim obj2 As MyClass = obj1

If obj1 Is obj2 Then
    Console.WriteLine("obj1 and obj2 are the same object.")
End If
```

This code will output that obj1 and obj2 are the same object since they reference the same instance.

3.5.5 Object Serialization

Serialization is the process of converting an object into a format that can be easily stored, transmitted, or reconstructed later. VB.NET provides serialization capabilities through libraries like XML Serialization and Binary Serialization.

Here's an example of XML serialization:

```
Imports System.Xml.Serialization

' Define a class for serialization
<Serializable()>
Public Class Person
    Public Property Name As String
End Class

' Serialize a Person object to XML
Dim person As New Person()
person.Name = "Alice"

Dim serializer As New XmlSerializer(GetType(Person))
Using writer As New StreamWriter("person.xml")
    serializer.Serialize(writer, person)
End Using
```

This code serializes a Person object to an XML file.

3.5.6 Object Disposal

In VB.NET, objects that implement the IDisposable interface require explicit disposal to release unmanaged resources, such as file handles or database connections. You should use the Using statement to ensure that the object is properly disposed of when it goes out of scope.

Here's an example using the FileStream class:

```
Using fs As New FileStream("example.txt", FileMode.Create)
    ' Perform operations with fs
End Using
```

In this code, the Using block ensures that the fs object is disposed of when the block is exited.

Working with objects is a fundamental aspect of VB.NET programming. Understanding how to create, access, initialize, compare, serialize, and dispose of objects is crucial for building robust and maintainable applications. VB.NET provides a wide range of tools and features to facilitate object-oriented programming and object management in your software projects.

Chapter 4: Graphical User Interface (GUI) Development

4.1 Creating Windows Forms Applications

Graphical User Interface (GUI) development is a crucial part of many software applications, providing users with an interactive and visual way to interact with the software. In this chapter, we will explore GUI development in VB.NET, focusing on Windows Forms applications.

4.1.1 Introduction to Windows Forms

Windows Forms, often abbreviated as WinForms, is a GUI framework for building Windows desktop applications. It provides a set of controls and components that allow you to create rich and interactive user interfaces. WinForms applications are event-driven, meaning they respond to user actions such as button clicks, mouse movements, and keyboard input.

4.1.2 Creating a Windows Forms Project

To create a Windows Forms project in VB.NET, follow these steps:

1. Open Visual Studio.
2. Click on "File" > "New" > "Project..."
3. In the "Create a new project" dialog, select "Windows Forms App (.NET Framework)" under "Visual Basic."
4. Enter a name for your project, choose a location, and click "Create."
5. Visual Studio will generate a default Windows Form called Form1.vb and display it in the designer.

4.1.3 The Visual Designer

The Visual Studio IDE includes a visual designer that simplifies the process of designing your Windows Forms user interface. You can drag and drop controls such as buttons, textboxes, labels, and more onto the form, and then use the properties window to customize their appearance and behavior.

4.1.4 Event Handling

WinForms applications are event-driven, and you can handle events generated by user interactions or other actions. For example, you can write code that responds to a button click event or a mouse movement event. To handle an event, you can double-click on a control in the designer, and Visual Studio will generate an event handler method for you.

Here's an example of handling a button click event:

```
Private Sub Button1_Click(sender As Object, e As EventArgs) Handles Button1.C
lick
    ' Code to execute when the button is clicked
```

```
    MessageBox.Show("Button clicked!")
End Sub
```

In this code, the `Button1_Click` method is called when `Button1` is clicked, and it displays a message box with the text "Button clicked!"

4.1.5 Running Your Application

To run your Windows Forms application, you can press the "Start" button in Visual Studio, or you can build the project and run the generated executable file. Your application will appear as a standalone Windows application with its own window, and users can interact with the controls you've placed on the form.

Windows Forms is a versatile framework for creating desktop applications in VB.NET. It offers a wide range of controls, event handling capabilities, and a visual designer that simplifies the development process. As you explore Windows Forms development further, you'll have the tools to create user-friendly and feature-rich desktop applications for various purposes.

4.2 Designing User Interfaces with WinForms

Designing user interfaces (UIs) is a critical aspect of Windows Forms (WinForms) development in VB.NET. A well-designed UI ensures that your application is user-friendly and intuitive. In this section, we'll explore various aspects of designing user interfaces using WinForms.

4.2.1 The Toolbox

The Toolbox is a crucial tool in the Visual Studio IDE for WinForms development. It provides a wide range of controls and components that you can drag and drop onto your Windows Form to create the UI. Common controls include buttons, textboxes, labels, checkboxes, radio buttons, and more.

To open the Toolbox, go to "View" > "Toolbox" in Visual Studio. You can then select the controls you need and add them to your form by clicking and dragging.

4.2.2 Layout and Alignment

Proper layout and alignment of controls are essential for creating a visually appealing and organized UI. WinForms provides several layout and alignment options, including containers like `Panel`, `GroupBox`, and `TableLayoutPanel` that help you arrange controls in a structured manner.

You can set properties like `Anchor` and `Dock` to control how controls resize and behave when the form is resized. The `Anchor` property specifies which edges of the control are anchored to the edges of the parent container, while the `Dock` property allows a control to fill the entire available space within its container.

4.2.3 Control Properties

Each control in WinForms has a set of properties that you can customize to control its appearance and behavior. For example, you can set the Text property of a Label to display a specific text, or the BackColor property of a Button to change its background color.

The Properties window in Visual Studio allows you to easily view and modify these properties for selected controls.

4.2.4 Event Handling

Event handling is a crucial part of UI design. You can write event handler methods to respond to user interactions with the UI elements. For example, you can write code to handle button clicks, text changes, mouse movements, and more.

To create an event handler, you can double-click on a control in the designer, and Visual Studio will generate the corresponding event handler method in your code. You can then add your custom logic to these event handlers.

4.2.5 Data Binding

Data binding is a feature in WinForms that allows you to connect UI elements, such as textboxes or grids, to data sources. This simplifies the process of displaying and updating data in your application's UI.

You can bind a control's property, such as the Text property of a textbox, to a data source, such as a database or a collection, and WinForms will automatically handle the data retrieval and updating.

4.2.6 Custom Controls

WinForms also allows you to create custom controls when the built-in controls do not meet your specific requirements. You can derive new controls from existing ones or create entirely custom controls that suit your application's unique needs.

Creating custom controls involves defining their appearance, behavior, and properties, and you can reuse these controls across multiple forms within your application.

4.2.7 Testing and Feedback

Testing is a critical step in UI design. You should thoroughly test your UI to ensure that it works as expected and is free of bugs or usability issues. Soliciting feedback from potential users can help you identify areas for improvement and make your UI more user-friendly.

Usability testing involves observing how users interact with your application and collecting feedback on their experience. It can lead to valuable insights for refining your UI design.

Designing user interfaces in WinForms requires a combination of creativity and attention to detail. A well-designed UI can significantly enhance the user experience of your application, making it more intuitive and efficient to use. As you gain experience in

WinForms development, you'll develop a better understanding of UI design principles and best practices that will help you create outstanding user interfaces for your applications.

4.3 Event-Driven Programming

Event-driven programming is a fundamental concept in Windows Forms (WinForms) development with VB.NET. It is the backbone of creating interactive and responsive user interfaces. In this section, we will delve into the principles of event-driven programming in WinForms.

4.3.1 Understanding Events

In the context of WinForms, an event is a specific action or occurrence that takes place during the execution of an application. Events can be generated by user interactions, such as clicking a button, moving the mouse, or pressing a key, or they can be triggered by system actions, like the form being loaded or closed.

Each control in WinForms can raise events, and you can write code to respond to these events. For example, a button control can raise a Click event, a textbox control can raise a TextChanged event, and a form can raise events like Load and Closing.

4.3.2 Event Handlers

Event handlers are methods in your VB.NET code that are executed in response to a specific event being raised. You can write event handler methods to specify what should happen when a particular event occurs.

In Visual Studio, you can create event handlers by double-clicking a control in the designer, and the IDE will generate the event handler method for you. Alternatively, you can manually create event handlers in your code and associate them with events using the Handles keyword.

Here's an example of an event handler for a button click event:

```
Private Sub Button1_Click(sender As Object, e As EventArgs) Handles Button1.Click
    ' Code to execute when Button1 is clicked
End Sub
```

In this code, the Button1_Click method will be called when Button1 is clicked, allowing you to define the actions to be taken in response to the click event.

4.3.3 Event Wiring

Event wiring is the process of connecting a control's event to an event handler. This linkage tells the control which method to call when a specific event occurs.

You can wire events in the Visual Studio designer by selecting a control, going to the Properties window, and clicking the lightning bolt icon to view and select the available events. Then, you can choose an event handler from the dropdown list or create a new one.

4.3.4 Event Parameters

Events can pass information to event handler methods through event parameters. These parameters provide context about the event, such as the sender of the event (the control that raised it) and any additional event-specific data.

For example, the Click event of a button passes two parameters: sender As Object and e As EventArgs. The sender parameter refers to the button that was clicked, and the e parameter contains event-specific information.

```
Private Sub Button1_Click(sender As Object, e As EventArgs) Handles Button1.C
lick
    Dim clickedButton As Button = DirectCast(sender, Button)
    MessageBox.Show($"Button '{clickedButton.Text}' was clicked.")
End Sub
```

In this code, we cast the sender parameter to a Button type to access properties of the clicked button.

4.3.5 Delegates and Event Types

Behind the scenes, events in WinForms are implemented using delegates, which are types that define the signature of event handler methods. Delegates allow multiple methods to be attached to an event.

For example, the Click event of a button is implemented using the EventHandler delegate, which has the following signature.

```
Private Sub Button1_Click(sender As Object, e As EventArgs)
```

In this signature, sender is of type Object, and e is of type EventArgs. The delegate ensures that any event handler method attached to the Click event has the same parameter types and return type.

Understanding event-driven programming is essential for creating responsive and interactive Windows Forms applications in VB.NET. By harnessing events, event handlers, and delegates, you can build applications that respond to user actions and system events effectively, providing a rich and engaging user experience.

4.4 Controls and Components

Controls and components are the building blocks of Windows Forms (WinForms) applications in VB.NET. In this section, we'll explore the fundamental controls and components that you can use to create the user interface and functionality of your WinForms applications.

WinForms provides a wide variety of common controls that you can use to create a rich user interface. Some of the most commonly used controls include:

- **Button**: Used for triggering actions or events when clicked.
- **Label**: Used for displaying text or a description.
- **Textbox**: Allows users to input and edit text.
- **Checkbox**: Provides binary options for selection.
- **Radio Button**: Used for selecting one option from a group.
- **List Box**: Displays a list of items for selection.
- **Combo Box**: Combines a textbox with a list box for item selection.
- **Picture Box**: Displays images.
- **Panel**: A container for grouping and organizing controls.
- **Group Box**: Provides a visual grouping of controls.
- **Tab Control**: Allows organizing controls into tabs.
- **Menu Strip**: Used for creating menus in the application.

These controls serve various purposes and are essential for designing the user interface of your WinForms application.

4.4.2 Container Controls

Container controls are controls that can host other controls. They are used for organizing and arranging controls within a form. Some common container controls include:

- **Panel**: A basic container for grouping controls together.
- **Group Box**: Similar to a panel but with a border and title.
- **FlowLayoutPanel**: Arranges controls in a flow-like manner.
- **TableLayoutPanel**: Organizes controls in rows and columns.
- **TabControl**: Allows multiple pages with different controls.

Container controls help maintain a structured layout and organization of controls within a form.

4.4.3 Custom Controls

While WinForms provides a wide range of built-in controls, there may be scenarios where you need to create custom controls tailored to your application's requirements. You can create custom controls by inheriting from existing controls or building entirely new controls from scratch.

Creating custom controls allows you to encapsulate complex functionality and reuse it across different forms or projects. Custom controls can be added to the Visual Studio Toolbox for easy drag-and-drop usage in the designer.

4.4.4 Component Classes

Components are non-visual elements that add functionality to your WinForms application. They are typically used for tasks such as data binding, data access, and error handling. Some commonly used component classes include:

- **Timer**: Allows you to execute code at specified intervals.
- **ErrorProvider**: Provides visual cues for error validation.
- **BindingSource**: Simplifies data binding between controls and data sources.
- **BackgroundWorker**: Enables asynchronous background tasks.
- **PrintDocument**: Supports printing documents and reports.
- **FileDialog**: Provides file dialog boxes for file operations.

Components are added to the form in the same way as controls and can be configured and utilized through properties and methods.

4.4.5 Custom Components

Similar to custom controls, you can also create custom components in VB.NET. Custom components encapsulate specific functionality that can be reused across different forms or projects. Custom components can be added to the Visual Studio Toolbox for easy integration into the designer.

Creating custom components is especially useful when you need to extend the capabilities of your WinForms application with specialized functionality that goes beyond the built-in components.

WinForms provides a rich ecosystem of controls and components that enable you to build versatile and feature-rich desktop applications. Whether you are working with common controls, container controls, custom controls, or components, understanding how to leverage these building blocks effectively is essential for creating user-friendly and functional WinForms applications.

4.5 Custom Controls and User Controls

Custom controls and user controls are essential components of Windows Forms (WinForms) development in VB.NET, allowing you to create reusable and specialized visual elements for your applications. In this section, we will explore the concepts of custom controls and user controls and how to create and use them effectively.

Before we dive into creating custom controls and user controls, let's distinguish between the two:

- **Custom Controls**: These are controls that you create by inheriting from existing WinForms controls or from the Control class directly. Custom controls offer a high degree of customization and can have complex behavior and appearance.

- **User Controls**: User controls are composite controls made by combining existing controls and components into a single reusable unit. They are essentially a collection of controls that are grouped together to provide a specific functionality or user interface element.

4.5.2 Creating Custom Controls

Creating a custom control involves creating a new class that inherits from an existing WinForms control or from the Control class itself. You can then override methods, define properties, and add event handlers to customize the behavior and appearance of the control.

Here's a simplified example of creating a custom button control that changes its text color when clicked:

```
Public Class CustomButton
    Inherits Button

    Public Sub New()
        ' Initialize the control's properties and behavior here.
        Me.Text = "Click Me"
    End Sub

    Protected Overrides Sub OnClick(e As EventArgs)
        ' Customize the behavior when the button is clicked.
        Me.ForeColor = Color.Red
        MyBase.OnClick(e)
    End Sub
End Class
```

You can use this custom button in your WinForms application like any other built-in control.

4.5.3 Creating User Controls

User controls are created by designing a visual interface in the WinForms designer and encapsulating it within a single component. To create a user control:

1. Right-click on your project in Solution Explorer and choose "Add" > "User Control."
2. Design the user interface of the control in the designer, adding buttons, textboxes, labels, and other controls as needed.

3. Add code-behind logic to the user control to handle events, perform actions, or provide additional functionality.

User controls are versatile and allow you to create complex, reusable components with ease. They are particularly useful when you need to package a group of controls and functionality into a single unit.

4.5.4 Benefits of Custom and User Controls

The benefits of using custom controls and user controls in your WinForms applications include:

- **Reusability**: You can use custom controls and user controls in multiple forms and projects, promoting code reusability and consistency.

- **Modularity**: Custom controls and user controls encapsulate functionality and UI elements, making your codebase modular and easier to maintain.

- **Customization**: You have full control over the appearance and behavior of custom controls, allowing you to tailor them to your specific needs.

- **Consistency**: User controls provide a way to ensure a consistent user interface and behavior across different parts of your application.

- **Abstraction**: Custom controls and user controls abstract complex functionality into easy-to-use components, simplifying development.

4.5.5 Using Custom and User Controls

To use a custom control or user control in your WinForms application, you can follow these general steps:

1. Build or design the custom control or user control.
2. Build your WinForms application.
3. In the toolbox, right-click and select "Choose Items."
4. In the "Choose Toolbox Items" dialog, click the "Browse" button and select the compiled assembly containing your custom control or user control.
5. The control should now appear in the toolbox and can be dragged and dropped onto your forms.

Once added to your form, you can set properties, handle events, and interact with custom controls and user controls just like any other WinForms control.

Custom controls and user controls are powerful tools for creating versatile and reusable components in WinForms applications. Whether you need to create specialized buttons, complex UI elements, or modular components, mastering the art of custom controls and user controls will enhance your ability to develop rich and maintainable desktop applications.

Chapter 5: Working with Data in VB.NET

5.1 Connecting to Databases

Working with data is a fundamental aspect of many applications, and VB.NET provides robust tools for connecting to databases, retrieving data, and performing data operations. In this section, we'll explore how to connect to databases in VB.NET and establish a foundation for data-related tasks.

5.1.1 Database Connection Basics

To interact with a database in VB.NET, you need to establish a connection to the database server. Common database systems include Microsoft SQL Server, MySQL, Oracle, and SQLite. VB.NET provides various database providers and connection options to work with different database systems.

Here's a basic example of connecting to a Microsoft SQL Server database using the ADO.NET library:

```
Imports System.Data.SqlClient

Public Class DatabaseConnector
    Private connectionString As String = "Data Source=ServerName;Initial Cata
log=DatabaseName;User ID=UserName;Password=Password"

    Public Sub ConnectToDatabase()
        Using connection As New SqlConnection(connectionString)
            Try
                connection.Open()
                ' Connection is established; you can perform database operati
ons here.
            Catch ex As Exception
                ' Handle connection error.
            End Try
        End Using
    End Sub
End Class
```

In this example, we use the SqlConnection class to establish a connection to the SQL Server database by providing the connection string, which contains server details and credentials.

5.1.2 Connection Strings

The connection string is a crucial component when connecting to a database. It contains information about the database server, database name, authentication credentials, and other settings required to establish a connection.

Connection strings may vary depending on the database system you are working with. It's essential to consult the documentation of the specific database provider you are using to construct the correct connection string.

5.1.3 Connection Pooling

VB.NET, along with ADO.NET, provides connection pooling, which is a mechanism for efficiently managing database connections. Connection pooling reuses existing connections rather than creating a new connection every time, improving performance and resource utilization.

By default, ADO.NET handles connection pooling automatically, so you do not need to manage it explicitly. You can open and close connections as needed, and ADO.NET will handle connection pooling behind the scenes.

5.1.4 Working with Different Database Providers

VB.NET supports a variety of database providers, each with its own set of classes and namespaces for interacting with databases. For example:

- For Microsoft SQL Server, you can use classes from the `System.Data.SqlClient` namespace.
- For MySQL, you can use the MySQL Connector/NET library.
- For Oracle, you can use the Oracle Data Provider for .NET (ODP.NET).
- For SQLite, you can use the System.Data.SQLite library.

You'll need to reference the appropriate libraries and namespaces in your VB.NET project to work with specific database systems.

5.1.5 Error Handling and Disposal

When working with database connections, it's essential to handle exceptions that may occur during the connection process. For example, network issues or incorrect credentials can result in connection failures. Proper error handling helps your application gracefully respond to such situations.

Additionally, it's good practice to use the `Using` statement or explicitly call the `Close` method to close the database connection when you are done with it. This ensures that resources are released promptly and efficiently.

```
Using connection As New SqlConnection(connectionString)
    Try
        connection.Open()
        ' Database operations here.
    Catch ex As Exception
        ' Handle connection error.
    Finally
        connection.Close()
    End Try
End Using
```

Connecting to databases is a fundamental step when working with data in VB.NET. Whether you are building applications that retrieve data, insert records, or perform complex database operations, understanding how to establish and manage database connections is a crucial skill. In the following sections of this chapter, we'll delve deeper into data access and manipulation techniques.

5.2 ADO.NET and Data Access

ADO.NET (ActiveX Data Objects for .NET) is a core technology for data access in VB.NET applications. It provides a set of classes and libraries that enable developers to connect to databases, retrieve and manipulate data, and work with data sources in a structured manner. In this section, we'll explore the fundamentals of ADO.NET and how to perform data access tasks.

5.2.1 Key ADO.NET Components

ADO.NET comprises several key components for data access:

- **Connection**: Represents a connection to a data source, such as a database server. It includes classes like `SqlConnection`, `OleDbConnection`, and `OracleConnection` for different database systems.

- **Command**: Used to execute SQL commands or stored procedures against a database. It includes classes like `SqlCommand`, `OleDbCommand`, and `OracleCommand`.

- **DataReader**: Provides a forward-only, read-only stream of data from a data source. It's efficient for retrieving large datasets.

- **DataAdapter**: Serves as a bridge between a dataset and a data source. It includes classes like `SqlDataAdapter`, `OleDbDataAdapter`, and `OracleDataAdapter`. Data adapters are commonly used for filling datasets and updating data sources.

- **DataSet**: Represents an in-memory, disconnected representation of data. It can hold multiple tables, relationships, and constraints. Datasets provide a convenient way to work with data offline.

5.2.2 Retrieving Data with DataReader

The `DataReader` is ideal for efficiently retrieving data from a database when you only need to read the data and don't intend to modify it. Here's an example of using a `DataReader` to fetch data from a SQL Server database:

```
Imports System.Data.SqlClient

Public Sub ReadDataFromDatabase()
    Dim connectionString As String = "Data Source=ServerName;Initial Catalog=
DatabaseName;User ID=UserName;Password=Password"
    Dim sql As String = "SELECT FirstName, LastName FROM Employees"
```

```
    Using connection As New SqlConnection(connectionString)
        connection.Open()

        Using command As New SqlCommand(sql, connection)
            Using reader As SqlDataReader = command.ExecuteReader()
                While reader.Read()
                    Dim firstName As String = reader.GetString(0)
                    Dim lastName As String = reader.GetString(1)
                    ' Process data here
                End While
            End Using
        End Using
    End Using
End Sub
```

In this example, we open a connection to the database, execute a SELECT query, and use the DataReader to loop through the results.

5.2.3 Working with DataSets and DataAdapters

DataSets and DataAdapters provide a more versatile approach to working with data. You can fill a DataSet with data from a database, manipulate it in memory, and then update changes back to the database. Here's a simplified example:

```
Imports System.Data.SqlClient

Public Sub FillAndUpdateDataSet()
    Dim connectionString As String = "Data Source=ServerName;Initial Catalog=
DatabaseName;User ID=UserName;Password=Password"
    Dim sql As String = "SELECT FirstName, LastName FROM Employees"

    Using connection As New SqlConnection(connectionString)
        connection.Open()

        Dim adapter As New SqlDataAdapter(sql, connection)
        Dim dataSet As New DataSet()

        ' Fill the DataSet with data from the database
        adapter.Fill(dataSet, "Employees")

        ' Modify data in the DataSet as needed
        Dim table As DataTable = dataSet.Tables("Employees")
        For Each row As DataRow In table.Rows
            ' Modify data in the DataRow
        Next

        ' Update changes back to the database
        adapter.Update(dataSet, "Employees")
```

```
        End Using
End Sub
```

In this example, we use a `SqlDataAdapter` to fill a DataSet with data, make changes to the DataSet, and then update those changes back to the database.

5.2.4 Parameterized Queries

When working with SQL queries, it's essential to use parameterized queries to prevent SQL injection attacks and improve code readability and maintainability. Here's an example of a parameterized query:

```
Imports System.Data.SqlClient

Public Sub ParameterizedQuery()
    Dim connectionString As String = "Data Source=ServerName;Initial Catalog=
DatabaseName;User ID=UserName;Password=Password"
    Dim sql As String = "SELECT FirstName, LastName FROM Employees WHERE Depa
rtment = @Dept"

    Using connection As New SqlConnection(connectionString)
        connection.Open()

        Using command As New SqlCommand(sql, connection)
            command.Parameters.AddWithValue("@Dept", "HR")

            Using reader As SqlDataReader = command.ExecuteReader()
                While reader.Read()
                    Dim firstName As String = reader.GetString(0)
                    Dim lastName As String = reader.GetString(1)
                    ' Process data here
                End While
            End Using
        End Using
    End Using
End Sub
```

In this example, we use the `SqlCommand.Parameters` collection to add parameters to the query, making it safe and efficient.

ADO.NET is a powerful framework for data access in VB.NET applications. Whether you're retrieving data with a DataReader, working with in-memory datasets, or using parameterized queries, ADO.NET provides the tools you need to interact with databases efficiently and securely. In the following sections, we'll explore more advanced data access techniques and data binding in VB.NET.

5.3 Data Binding and Display

Data binding is a powerful feature in VB.NET that allows you to connect user interface elements, such as controls in a Windows Form, to data sources like databases, collections, or objects. Data binding simplifies the process of displaying, editing, and synchronizing data between the user interface and data sources. In this section, we'll explore the concepts of data binding in VB.NET.

5.3.1 Data Binding Basics

At its core, data binding establishes a connection between a control's property (such as the text property of a textbox) and a data source. When data binding is set up, changes made to the control or the data source are automatically synchronized. This eliminates the need for manual updates and ensures that the user interface reflects the latest data.

To perform data binding in VB.NET, follow these basic steps:

1. **Choose a Data Source**: Select the data source you want to bind to. This can be a database, a collection, an object, or any other data structure.

2. **Choose a Control**: Select the control on your form that you want to bind to the data source. For example, you can bind a textbox to a field in a database table.

3. **Set Data Binding Properties**: Configure the data binding properties of the control. This typically involves specifying the data source, data member (the specific data field or property), and binding mode.

4. **Binding Expressions**: In some cases, you may use binding expressions to format or manipulate the data before it's displayed. Binding expressions are written in a specific syntax and can be used in data-bound controls like labels or textboxes.

5.3.2 Data Binding Modes

VB.NET supports several data binding modes that determine how data is synchronized between the control and the data source. Common data binding modes include:

- **One-Way**: Data flows in one direction, from the data source to the control. Changes in the data source are reflected in the control, but changes in the control don't affect the data source.

- **Two-Way**: Data flows in both directions, allowing changes in the control to update the data source and vice versa. This is useful for creating forms that can both display and edit data.

- **One-Way to Source**: Data flows from the control to the data source, allowing changes in the control to update the data source, but changes in the data source do not affect the control. This mode is less common but can be useful in specific scenarios.

5.3.3 Example of Data Binding

Here's a simplified example of data binding in VB.NET:

```vbnet
Imports System.Windows.Forms

Public Class MainForm
    Private customers As New List(Of Customer)

    Public Sub New()
        ' Initialize the form and data source
        InitializeComponent()
        customers.Add(New Customer("John", "Doe"))
        customers.Add(New Customer("Jane", "Smith"))

        ' Bind the ListBox to the customers list
        listBoxCustomers.DataSource = customers
        listBoxCustomers.DisplayMember = "FullName"
    End Sub
End Class

Public Class Customer
    Public Property FirstName As String
    Public Property LastName As String

    Public ReadOnly Property FullName As String
        Get
            Return $"{FirstName} {LastName}"
        End Get
    End Property

    Public Sub New(firstName As String, lastName As String)
        Me.FirstName = firstName
        Me.LastName = lastName
    End Sub
End Class
```

In this example, we create a Windows Form with a ListBox control. We bind the ListBox to a list of Customer objects, and we specify that the FullName property should be displayed in the ListBox. As a result, the ListBox will automatically display the full names of customers, and changes to the list of customers will be reflected in the ListBox.

5.3.4 Data Binding in Windows Forms

Windows Forms (WinForms) provides a rich set of data-bound controls that simplify data binding. Some commonly used data-bound controls include DataGridView (for displaying tabular data), ListBox, ComboBox, TextBox, and Label.

You can use the Visual Studio designer to set up data binding visually, or you can perform data binding programmatically in code, as shown in the example above.

Data binding is a valuable tool in VB.NET for creating responsive and data-driven user interfaces. It simplifies the process of connecting controls to data sources and ensures that your application's user interface always reflects the latest data. Whether you're building desktop applications or complex data-driven forms, mastering data binding is essential for efficient and effective development.

5.4 Working with LINQ

Language-Integrated Query (LINQ) is a powerful feature in VB.NET that allows you to query and manipulate collections of objects, databases, XML documents, and other data sources using a consistent and expressive syntax. LINQ makes it easier to work with data and provides a more readable and maintainable way to write queries. In this section, we'll explore the basics of working with LINQ in VB.NET.

5.4.1 LINQ Query Syntax

LINQ offers two primary syntaxes for writing queries: query syntax and method syntax. Query syntax resembles SQL-like statements and is often used for readability. Method syntax, on the other hand, uses method calls to construct queries and is more concise. Both syntaxes are functionally equivalent, so you can choose the one that best fits your coding style and requirements.

Here's an example of LINQ query syntax to filter a list of integers:

```
Dim numbers As List(Of Integer) = New List(Of Integer) From {1, 2, 3, 4, 5, 6
, 7, 8, 9, 10}

Dim evenNumbers = From num In numbers
                  Where num Mod 2 = 0
                  Select num
```

In this query, we use the From clause to specify the data source (numbers list), the Where clause to filter even numbers, and the Select clause to project the results.

5.4.2 LINQ Method Syntax

The same query can be expressed using LINQ method syntax as follows:

```
Dim numbers As List(Of Integer) = New List(Of Integer) From {1, 2, 3, 4, 5, 6
, 7, 8, 9, 10}

Dim evenNumbers = numbers.Where(Function(num) num Mod 2 = 0).Select(Function(
num) num)
```

In method syntax, we use the Where method to filter and the Select method to project the results. Lambda expressions define the conditions and projections.

5.4.3 LINQ to Objects

LINQ can be used to query in-memory collections, such as arrays, lists, or dictionaries. LINQ to Objects provides a powerful way to filter, sort, and transform data without writing extensive loops and conditions.

Here's an example of sorting a list of strings using LINQ:

```
Dim fruits As List(Of String) = New List(Of String) From {"Apple", "Banana",
"Cherry", "Date", "Fig"}

Dim sortedFruits = From fruit In fruits
                   Order By fruit
                   Select fruit
```

In this query, the Order By clause is used to sort the fruits list alphabetically.

5.4.4 LINQ to SQL

LINQ to SQL is an ORM (Object-Relational Mapping) technology that allows you to query and manipulate relational databases using LINQ. It provides a mapping between database tables and .NET objects, making it easy to work with databases in an object-oriented manner.

Here's an example of querying a SQL Server database using LINQ to SQL:

```
Dim db As New YourDataContext() ' Create an instance of your LINQ to SQL Data
Context
Dim employees = From emp In db.Employees
                Where emp.Department = "HR"
                Select emp
```

In this example, we query the Employees table in the database and filter employees by their department.

5.4.5 LINQ to XML

LINQ to XML allows you to query and manipulate XML documents using LINQ. It provides a convenient way to traverse XML structures, filter elements, and create XML documents programmatically.

Here's an example of querying an XML document using LINQ to XML:

```
Dim xml As XElement = XElement.Load("sample.xml")

Dim books = From book In xml.<library>.<book>
            Where book.@category = "Science Fiction"
            Select book
```

In this query, we load an XML document and query for books in the "Science Fiction" category.

LINQ is a versatile and expressive feature in VB.NET that simplifies data querying and manipulation. Whether you're working with in-memory collections, databases, or XML documents, LINQ provides a consistent and readable way to interact with data. By mastering LINQ, you can improve the efficiency and maintainability of your code when dealing with various data sources.

5.5 Advanced Data Access Techniques

While the fundamentals of data access in VB.NET involve connecting to databases, querying data, and performing basic operations, there are several advanced techniques and concepts that can enhance your data access capabilities. In this section, we'll explore some of these advanced data access techniques.

5.5.1 Entity Framework (EF)

Entity Framework is an Object-Relational Mapping (ORM) framework that simplifies database access in VB.NET applications. It provides a higher-level abstraction over ADO.NET and allows you to work with databases using .NET objects and LINQ queries. EF includes features like automatic code generation, change tracking, and support for various database providers.

Here's a simplified example of using Entity Framework to query a database:

```
Using context As New YourDbContext()
    Dim employees = From emp In context.Employees
                    Where emp.Department = "HR"
                    Select emp
End Using
```

Entity Framework simplifies database operations by eliminating the need to write SQL queries and providing a more intuitive way to work with data.

5.5.2 Stored Procedures

Stored procedures are precompiled database queries stored on the database server. They offer performance benefits and security advantages. VB.NET allows you to call stored procedures using ADO.NET or Entity Framework.

Here's an example of calling a stored procedure using ADO.NET:

```
Using connection As New SqlConnection(connectionString)
    connection.Open()

    Using command As New SqlCommand("YourStoredProcedure", connection)
        command.CommandType = CommandType.StoredProcedure

        ' Add parameters if needed
        command.Parameters.AddWithValue("@ParameterName", parameterValue)
```

```
        Using reader As SqlDataReader = command.ExecuteReader()
            ' Process the results
        End Using
    End Using
End Using
```

A Data Access Layer (DAL) is an architectural pattern that separates data access code from the rest of your application. It provides a structured way to interact with databases and encapsulates database-specific logic. You can create a DAL in VB.NET to centralize data access operations and promote code reusability.

Here's a simplified example of a DAL method:

```
Public Class EmployeeDAL
    Private connectionString As String = "YourConnectionString"

    Public Function GetEmployeesByDepartment(department As String) As List(Of
Employee)
        Dim employees As New List(Of Employee)

        Using connection As New SqlConnection(connectionString)
            connection.Open()

            Using command As New SqlCommand("SELECT * FROM Employees WHERE De
partment = @Dept", connection)
                command.Parameters.AddWithValue("@Dept", department)

                Using reader As SqlDataReader = command.ExecuteReader()
                    While reader.Read()
                        Dim employee As New Employee()
                        ' Map data from the reader to the Employee object
                        employees.Add(employee)
                    End While
                End Using
            End Using
        End Using

        Return employees
    End Function
End Class
```

Several data access patterns, such as Repository Pattern and Unit of Work Pattern, provide higher-level abstractions for working with databases. These patterns promote separation of concerns, testability, and maintainability in your codebase. You can implement these patterns in VB.NET applications to manage data access operations more effectively.

5.5.5 Caching and Performance Optimization

Caching is a technique that can significantly improve the performance of data-intensive applications. VB.NET provides caching mechanisms that allow you to store frequently accessed data in memory, reducing the need to query the database repeatedly. Caching can be implemented using libraries like System.Runtime.Caching or third-party caching solutions.

Advanced data access techniques in VB.NET offer solutions to complex data access scenarios, improve code organization, and enhance the overall performance and maintainability of your applications. By leveraging Entity Framework, stored procedures, Data Access Layers, and design patterns, you can build robust and efficient data access solutions tailored to your project's requirements. Additionally, caching strategies can further optimize the performance of your applications by reducing database load and response times.

Chapter 6: File Handling and Input/Output Operations

6.1 Reading and Writing Files

File handling is a fundamental aspect of many software applications, and in VB.NET, you have powerful tools and libraries to work with files. This section covers the basics of reading and writing files in VB.NET.

Reading Files

To read data from a file in VB.NET, you typically follow these steps:

1. **Specify the File Path:** You need to provide the path to the file you want to read. This can be an absolute or relative path.

2. **Open the File:** Use the StreamReader class to open the file for reading. This class provides methods to read text or binary data from a file.

3. **Read Data:** Use methods like ReadLine() or ReadToEnd() to read the content of the file. You can read data line by line or as a whole, depending on your needs.

4. **Close the File:** Always close the file when you're done reading it to free up system resources.

Here's an example of reading text from a file:

```
Dim filePath As String = "C:\example.txt"

Using reader As New StreamReader(filePath)
    Dim line As String
    While Not reader.EndOfStream
        line = reader.ReadLine()
        ' Process the line of text
    End While
End Using
```

Writing Files

To write data to a file in VB.NET, you typically follow these steps:

1. **Specify the File Path:** Similar to reading, you need to specify the path to the file you want to write. If the file doesn't exist, it will be created.

2. **Open the File:** Use the StreamWriter class to open the file for writing. This class provides methods to write text or binary data to a file.

3. **Write Data:** Use methods like Write(), WriteLine(), or WriteAsync() to write data to the file.

4. **Close the File:** Always close the file when you're done writing to ensure data is flushed and the file is properly closed.

Here's an example of writing text to a file:

```vbnet
Dim filePath As String = "C:\output.txt"

Using writer As New StreamWriter(filePath)
    writer.WriteLine("Hello, VB.NET!")
    writer.WriteLine("This is a sample text.")
End Using
```

Handling Exceptions

When working with files, it's important to handle exceptions, such as file not found, permissions issues, or disk full errors. You can use Try...Catch blocks to gracefully handle these exceptions and provide appropriate error messages or actions.

File handling in VB.NET is flexible and can be used for various purposes, from reading and writing configuration files to processing large data files. It's essential to follow best practices and ensure proper error handling to create robust file handling code.

6.2 Stream-Based File Operations

In addition to the StreamReader and StreamWriter classes for text-based file operations, VB.NET provides stream-based file operations that allow you to work with files at a lower level. Streams are more versatile and can handle both text and binary data. In this section, we'll explore stream-based file operations in VB.NET.

Streams and File Operations

A stream is a sequence of bytes that can be read from or written to a file. Streams are a low-level way to work with files and provide greater flexibility than text-based operations.

Here are the key components of stream-based file operations:

*   **Stream:** Represents the data source or destination, such as a file, memory, or network connection. In VB.NET, you can use various stream classes like FileStream, MemoryStream, and NetworkStream.

*   **Reading:** To read data from a file, you create a stream for reading and use methods like Read() or ReadAsync() to retrieve data.

*   **Writing:** To write data to a file, you create a stream for writing and use methods like Write() or WriteAsync() to send data.

Reading Files with Streams

Here's an example of reading a file using a FileStream:

```
Dim filePath As String = "C:\example.txt"

Using stream As New FileStream(filePath, FileMode.Open, FileAccess.Read)
    Dim buffer As Byte() = New Byte(1024) {}
    Dim bytesRead As Integer

    Do
        bytesRead = stream.Read(buffer, 0, buffer.Length)
        If bytesRead > 0 Then
            ' Process the data in the buffer
        End If
    Loop While bytesRead > 0
End Using
```

In this example, we open a file using `FileStream` in read mode, read data into a buffer, and process the data as needed.

Writing Files with Streams

Here's an example of writing to a file using a `FileStream`:

```
Dim filePath As String = "C:\output.txt"

Using stream As New FileStream(filePath, FileMode.Create, FileAccess.Write)
    Dim data As Byte() = Encoding.UTF8.GetBytes("Hello, VB.NET!")
    stream.Write(data, 0, data.Length)
End Using
```

In this example, we open a file using `FileStream` in write mode, convert text to bytes using the `Encoding` class, and write the data to the file.

Binary File Operations

Streams are versatile and can handle binary data as well. You can read and write binary files, such as image files or serialized objects, using stream-based operations. The key is to use appropriate methods to read and write binary data.

```
Dim filePath As String = "C:\image.jpg"

Using stream As New FileStream(filePath, FileMode.Open, FileAccess.Read)
    Dim buffer As Byte() = New Byte(1024) {}
    Dim bytesRead As Integer

    Do
        bytesRead = stream.Read(buffer, 0, buffer.Length)
        If bytesRead > 0 Then
            ' Process binary data in the buffer
        End If
    Loop While bytesRead > 0
End Using
```

In this example, we read a binary image file using a `FileStream`.

Stream-based file operations provide fine-grained control over file access and are suitable for working with various types of data, including text and binary. Whether you're processing text files or dealing with complex binary formats, streams offer the flexibility and efficiency needed for file manipulation in VB.NET.

6.3 Serialization and Deserialization

Serialization and deserialization are essential techniques in VB.NET for converting complex data structures, such as objects, into a format that can be easily stored, transmitted, or persisted, and then restored back to their original form. This section explores how to perform serialization and deserialization in VB.NET.

Serialization

Serialization is the process of converting an object's state into a byte stream. This byte stream can be saved to a file, sent over a network, or stored in a database. In VB.NET, you can use the `BinaryFormatter` or `DataContractSerializer` for object serialization.

Here's an example of object serialization using `BinaryFormatter`:

```
Imports System.IO
Imports System.Runtime.Serialization.Formatters.Binary

' Create an instance of the object to be serialized
Dim person As New Person()
person.Name = "John"
person.Age = 30

' Create a FileStream to write the serialized data to a file
Dim filePath As String = "person.dat"
Using fs As FileStream = New FileStream(filePath, FileMode.Create)
    Dim formatter As New BinaryFormatter()

    ' Serialize the object to the file
    formatter.Serialize(fs, person)
End Using
```

In this example, we create an instance of the `Person` class and serialize it to a binary file using `BinaryFormatter`. The object's state, including its properties, is saved to the file.

Deserialization

Deserialization is the reverse process of taking a byte stream and converting it back into an object. In VB.NET, you can use the same serializers mentioned earlier (e.g., `BinaryFormatter` or `DataContractSerializer`) for deserialization.

Here's an example of object deserialization using `BinaryFormatter`:

```vb
Imports System.IO
Imports System.Runtime.Serialization.Formatters.Binary

' Create a FileStream to read the serialized data from a file
Dim filePath As String = "person.dat"
Using fs As FileStream = New FileStream(filePath, FileMode.Open)
    Dim formatter As New BinaryFormatter()

    ' Deserialize the object from the file
    Dim person As Person = DirectCast(formatter.Deserialize(fs), Person)

    ' Access the deserialized object's properties
    Console.WriteLine($"Name: {person.Name}, Age: {person.Age}")
End Using
```

In this example, we read the serialized data from the file and use `BinaryFormatter` to deserialize it back into a `Person` object. This allows us to access and work with the object's properties.

Serialization Best Practices

When performing serialization in VB.NET, consider the following best practices:

- Ensure that the classes you want to serialize are marked as `[Serializable]` or implement the `ISerializable` interface.

- Be cautious when deserializing data from untrusted sources, as it can potentially execute malicious code. Implement security measures, such as using a custom serialization binder or validation.

Serialization and deserialization are valuable techniques for persisting and transmitting complex data structures. They are commonly used in scenarios like saving application state, sharing data between different platforms, and storing data in databases. Understanding how to serialize and deserialize objects is a crucial skill for VB.NET developers.

6.4 Working with XML Data

XML (Extensible Markup Language) is a widely used format for storing and exchanging structured data. In VB.NET, you can work with XML data using various classes from the `System.Xml` namespace. This section explores how to work with XML data, including reading and writing XML files, parsing XML, and manipulating XML documents.

Reading XML Data

To read XML data from a file or a stream, you can use the `XmlReader` class, which provides a forward-only, read-only cursor for traversing XML documents. Here's an example of reading XML data from a file:

```
Imports System.Xml

' Create an XmlReader for the XML file
Dim filePath As String = "data.xml"
Using reader As XmlReader = XmlReader.Create(filePath)
    While reader.Read()
        ' Check the node type
        If reader.NodeType = XmlNodeType.Element AndAlso reader.Name = "Perso
n" Then
            ' Read and process XML elements
            Dim name As String = reader.GetAttribute("Name")
            Dim age As Integer = Integer.Parse(reader.GetAttribute("Age"))
            ' Process the data as needed
        End If
    End While
End Using
```

In this example, we use an `XmlReader` to read XML data from the "data.xml" file. As we traverse the XML, we check for specific elements and attributes and process the data accordingly.

Writing XML Data

To create and write XML data, you can use the `XmlWriter` class. This class allows you to generate XML documents programmatically. Here's an example of writing XML data to a file:

```
Imports System.Xml

' Create an XmlWriter to write XML to a file
Dim filePath As String = "output.xml"
Dim settings As New XmlWriterSettings()
settings.Indent = True

Using writer As XmlWriter = XmlWriter.Create(filePath, settings)
    ' Start writing the XML document
    writer.WriteStartDocument()

    ' Write the root element
    writer.WriteStartElement("People")

    ' Write individual person elements
    writer.WriteStartElement("Person")
    writer.WriteAttributeString("Name", "John")
```

```vbnet
    writer.WriteAttributeString("Age", "30")
    writer.WriteEndElement()

    ' Write more person elements as needed

    ' End the root element
    writer.WriteEndElement()

    ' End the XML document
    writer.WriteEndDocument()
End Using
```

In this example, we use an XmlWriter to create an XML document. We specify settings to make the output human-readable. We then write XML elements and attributes to create the desired structure.

Manipulating XML Documents

To manipulate XML documents, you can use the XmlDocument class. It provides a DOM (Document Object Model) representation of the XML, allowing you to navigate, modify, and query the document easily. Here's a simplified example of loading and manipulating an XML document:

```vbnet
Imports System.Xml

' Load an existing XML document
Dim doc As New XmlDocument()
doc.Load("data.xml")

' Find and modify elements
Dim personNode As XmlNode = doc.SelectSingleNode("/People/Person[@Name='John'
]")
If personNode IsNot Nothing Then
    Dim ageNode As XmlNode = personNode.SelectSingleNode("@Age")
    ageNode.Value = "31"
End If

' Save the modified document
doc.Save("data.xml")
```

In this example, we load an existing XML document, find a specific element using XPath, and modify its attribute value. Finally, we save the modified document back to the same file.

Working with XML data is common in various scenarios, including configuration files, data exchange, and web services. VB.NET provides robust support for XML handling, allowing you to parse, create, and manipulate XML documents efficiently.

6.5 Interacting with External Files and Devices

In VB.NET, you often need to interact with external files and devices to perform various tasks, such as reading data from sensors, controlling hardware peripherals, or managing files and directories on the file system. This section explores how to interact with external files and devices using VB.NET.

Working with Files and Directories

VB.NET provides a rich set of classes in the System.IO namespace for working with files and directories. You can perform operations such as creating, deleting, copying, moving, and renaming files and directories. Here are some common file and directory operations:

```vb
' Check if a file exists
Dim filePath As String = "example.txt"
If File.Exists(filePath) Then
    ' Perform operations on the file
End If

' Create a directory
Directory.CreateDirectory("NewFolder")

' Delete a file
File.Delete(filePath)

' Copy a file
File.Copy("source.txt", "destination.txt", True)

' Move or rename a file
File.Move("oldName.txt", "newName.txt")

' Get file information
Dim fileInfo As New FileInfo(filePath)
Console.WriteLine($"File Name: {fileInfo.Name}, File Size: {fileInfo.Length}
bytes")

' Enumerate files in a directory
Dim files As String() = Directory.GetFiles("C:\Directory")
```

Serial Communication

For communicating with external devices via serial ports (e.g., COM ports), you can use the System.IO.Ports namespace. Serial communication is often used in scenarios like connecting to microcontrollers, sensors, or other hardware devices. Here's a simplified example of reading data from a serial port:

```vbnet
Imports System.IO.Ports

Dim serialPort As New SerialPort("COM1", 9600) ' COM port and baud rate
serialPort.Open() ' Open the serial port

AddHandler serialPort.DataReceived, Sub(sender, e)
    ' Read data when data is received
    Dim data As String = serialPort.ReadLine()
    Console.WriteLine($"Received Data: {data}")
End Sub

' Keep the application running
Console.WriteLine("Press Enter to exit...")
Console.ReadLine()

' Close the serial port when done
serialPort.Close()
```

In this example, we open a serial port, define an event handler to read data when it's received, and keep the application running until the user presses Enter. Finally, we close the serial port when done.

Working with External Devices

Interfacing with external devices often involves using device-specific libraries or APIs. Whether you're working with USB devices, sensors, or custom hardware, you'll need to understand the device's communication protocol and use the appropriate libraries or drivers.

VB.NET provides the flexibility to interact with external files and devices, making it suitable for a wide range of applications, from desktop software to embedded systems. When working with external devices, it's essential to have a good understanding of the device's specifications and communication protocols to ensure successful integration with your VB.NET applications.

Chapter 7: Exception Handling and Error Management

Exception handling is a critical aspect of software development in VB.NET. It allows you to gracefully handle unexpected or exceptional situations that may occur during the execution of your application. This chapter delves into the fundamentals of exception handling and best practices for error management.

7.1 Understanding Exceptions

An exception is an abnormal condition or event that occurs during the execution of a program and disrupts the normal flow of instructions. Exceptions can be caused by various factors, such as invalid input, resource unavailability, or unexpected runtime errors. VB.NET provides a robust exception handling mechanism to identify, handle, and recover from these exceptional situations.

The Exception Hierarchy

In VB.NET, exceptions are organized into a hierarchy of classes. At the top of this hierarchy is the System.Exception class, which serves as the base class for all exceptions. Derived from System.Exception are various exception classes that represent specific types of exceptions, such as System.NullReferenceException, System.IO.IOException, or System.DividedByZeroException. These exception classes provide valuable information about the type and cause of the exception.

Throwing Exceptions

In VB.NET, you can intentionally throw exceptions using the Throw statement. Throwing an exception allows you to indicate that something unexpected or erroneous has occurred within your code. You can throw exceptions with or without specifying a particular exception type.

Here's an example of throwing a custom exception:

```
Sub Divide(ByVal dividend As Integer, ByVal divisor As Integer)
    If divisor = 0 Then
        Throw New DivideByZeroException("Division by zero is not allowed.")
    Else
        Dim result As Double = dividend / divisor
        Console.WriteLine($"Result: {result}")
    End If
End Sub
```

In this example, if the divisor is zero, we intentionally throw a DivideByZeroException with a custom error message. Otherwise, we perform the division operation.

To handle exceptions in VB.NET, you use the Try-Catch construct. The Try block contains the code that may throw exceptions, and the Catch block(s) handle those exceptions. Multiple Catch blocks can be used to catch different types of exceptions.

```
Try
    ' Code that may throw exceptions
    Dim result As Double = 10 / 0
    Console.WriteLine($"Result: {result}")
Catch ex As DivideByZeroException
    ' Handle DivideByZeroException
    Console.WriteLine("Division by zero is not allowed.")
Catch ex As Exception
    ' Handle other exceptions
    Console.WriteLine($"An error occurred: {ex.Message}")
End Try
```

In this example, the Try block attempts to perform a division by zero, which results in a DivideByZeroException. The first Catch block handles this specific exception, while the second Catch block serves as a catch-all for other exceptions.

Exception handling allows your application to gracefully respond to errors and prevent crashes. Understanding the exception hierarchy, throwing exceptions when necessary, and effectively using the Try-Catch construct are essential skills for robust error management in VB.NET applications.

7.2 Try-Catch Blocks

The Try-Catch construct is a fundamental part of VB.NET's exception handling mechanism. It allows you to handle exceptions gracefully, ensuring that your application can recover from unexpected errors and continue its operation or provide helpful feedback to the user.

The Structure of Try-Catch Blocks

A Try-Catch block consists of the following parts:

1. **Try Block**: This is where you place the code that might throw exceptions. The code within the Try block is monitored for exceptions.

2. **Catch Blocks**: These follow the Try block and are used to catch and handle specific exceptions. You can have one or more Catch blocks, each targeting a specific exception type. The first Catch block that matches the thrown exception's type will handle it.

3. **Finally Block (Optional)**: The Finally block is executed whether or not an exception is thrown. It is typically used to clean up resources or perform actions that must happen regardless of whether an exception occurred.

Here's an example of a simple `Try-Catch` block:

```
Try
    ' Code that may throw exceptions
    Dim result As Double = 10 / 0
    Console.WriteLine($"Result: {result}")
Catch ex As DivideByZeroException
    ' Handle DivideByZeroException
    Console.WriteLine("Division by zero is not allowed.")
Catch ex As Exception
    ' Handle other exceptions
    Console.WriteLine($"An error occurred: {ex.Message}")
Finally
    ' Clean up resources or perform necessary tasks
    Console.WriteLine("Finally block executed.")
End Try
```

In this example, the `Try` block contains code that attempts to perform a division by zero, which results in a `DivideByZeroException`. The first `Catch` block handles this specific exception, displaying an error message. The `Finally` block is executed afterward, even if no exception occurred.

Multiple Catch Blocks

You can have multiple `Catch` blocks to handle different types of exceptions. The order of `Catch` blocks is important because the first one that matches the thrown exception type will handle it. More specific exception types should come before more general ones.

```
Try
    ' Code that may throw exceptions
Catch ex As DivideByZeroException
    ' Handle DivideByZeroException
Catch ex As ArithmeticException
    ' Handle other arithmetic exceptions
Catch ex As Exception
    ' Handle all other exceptions
End Try
```

In this example, if a `DivideByZeroException` occurs, the first `Catch` block will handle it. If an `ArithmeticException` other than `DivideByZeroException` occurs, the second `Catch` block will handle it. All other exceptions will be caught by the third `Catch` block.

Using Exception Objects

Inside a `Catch` block, you can access information about the exception using the ex variable (or any other variable name you choose). This object provides properties like `Message` (containing the error message), `StackTrace` (containing the call stack information), and `InnerException` (containing information about any inner exception if applicable).

```
Catch ex As Exception
    Console.WriteLine($"An error occurred: {ex.Message}")
    Console.WriteLine($"StackTrace: {ex.StackTrace}")
    If ex.InnerException IsNot Nothing Then
        Console.WriteLine($"Inner Exception: {ex.InnerException.Message}")
    End If
End Try
```

This allows you to log or display useful information about the exception for debugging or user feedback.

The `Try-Catch` construct is crucial for managing exceptions effectively in VB.NET applications. It enables you to handle errors gracefully, preventing crashes and ensuring a better user experience.

7.3 Custom Exceptions

While VB.NET provides a wide range of built-in exception classes for handling common error scenarios, there are situations where you may need to create custom exceptions to represent specific errors or conditions that are unique to your application. This section explores the creation and use of custom exceptions in VB.NET.

Why Use Custom Exceptions?

Custom exceptions allow you to provide more meaningful and specific information about errors that occur in your application. They also help in organizing and categorizing exceptions based on your application's requirements. Some common reasons for creating custom exceptions include:

1. **Semantic Clarity**: Custom exceptions can have names that reflect the specific error or issue, making the code more self-explanatory.

2. **Categorization**: You can group related exceptions under a common base exception class, making it easier to catch and handle them as a group.

3. **Additional Information**: Custom exceptions can carry additional data or context about the error, which can be useful for debugging or logging.

Creating Custom Exceptions

In VB.NET, creating a custom exception involves creating a new class that inherits from the `System.Exception` class or one of its derived classes. You can add additional properties or methods to your custom exception class to provide more information about the error.

Here's an example of a custom exception class:

```
Public Class CustomApplicationException
    Inherits Exception
```

```vbnet
    Public Sub New(message As String)
        MyBase.New(message)
    End Sub

    Public Sub New(message As String, innerException As Exception)
        MyBase.New(message, innerException)
    End Sub

    Public Property ErrorCode As Integer
End Class
```

In this example, we create a custom exception class named `CustomApplicationException` that inherits from `System.Exception`. It has two constructors, allowing us to specify a custom error message and an inner exception. Additionally, it includes a property `ErrorCode` to store additional information about the error.

Throwing and Catching Custom Exceptions

Once you've defined a custom exception class, you can throw it within your code when a specific error condition is encountered:

```vbnet
Sub PerformOperation()
    Try
        ' Some code that may raise a custom exception
        Throw New CustomApplicationException("An error occurred in the operat
ion.")
    Catch ex As CustomApplicationException
        ' Handle the custom exception
        Console.WriteLine($"Custom Exception: {ex.Message}, ErrorCode: {ex.Er
rorCode}")
    Catch ex As Exception
        ' Handle other exceptions
        Console.WriteLine($"An error occurred: {ex.Message}")
    End Try
End Sub
```

In this example, when the `PerformOperation` function is called, it throws a `CustomApplicationException`. We catch this custom exception in a specific `Catch` block where we can access its properties like `Message` and `ErrorCode`.

Using Custom Exceptions for Contextual Information

Custom exceptions can also be useful for providing contextual information about the error. For instance, you can include details like the method or module where the exception occurred, the input parameters, or any relevant state information. This can greatly aid in debugging and troubleshooting.

Custom exceptions are a powerful tool for improving the clarity and manageability of your code when dealing with exceptional situations. By creating and using custom exceptions effectively, you can make your application's error handling more precise and informative.

7.4 Logging and Error Reporting

Logging and error reporting are essential aspects of exception handling and application maintenance. In this section, we'll explore techniques for logging and reporting errors in your VB.NET applications.

The Importance of Logging

Logging involves recording information about the application's execution, including any errors or exceptions that occur. Logging serves several purposes:

1. **Debugging**: Logs provide a detailed record of the application's behavior, making it easier to identify and resolve issues during development and testing.

2. **Monitoring**: In production environments, logs allow you to monitor the application's health and performance. You can detect and respond to errors or anomalies in real-time.

3. **Auditing**: Logs can be used for auditing purposes to track user actions, system events, and security-related activities.

4. **Error Reporting**: Logs help in error reporting and diagnostics. They provide valuable information about the context and cause of errors, making it easier to fix issues reported by users.

Logging Frameworks

VB.NET developers often rely on logging frameworks to simplify the process of capturing and managing log information. Popular logging frameworks for .NET include:

- **Log4Net**: A widely-used open-source logging framework that provides extensive configuration options and supports various output formats, such as files, databases, or event logs.

- **NLog**: Another popular open-source logging framework with similar features to Log4Net, offering flexibility and extensibility.

- **Serilog**: A newer logging framework known for its structured logging capabilities, allowing you to log structured data in a variety of formats.

These logging frameworks provide convenient ways to configure and control log output, including log levels (e.g., info, warning, error), log destinations, and log formatting.

To use a logging framework in your VB.NET application, you typically follow these steps:

1. **Install the Logging Framework**: Use NuGet Package Manager to add the logging framework library to your project.

2. **Configure Logging**: Configure the logging framework by specifying settings such as log destination (file, database, console), log level, and log format. Configuration can be done in code or through configuration files.

3. **Add Logging Statements**: Within your code, insert logging statements at relevant locations to record important events, such as the start and end of methods, exceptions, and significant application events.

Here's an example of configuring and using the Log4Net logging framework:

```vbnet
' Install Log4Net via NuGet Package Manager

' Configure Log4Net (typically in an application startup method)
XmlConfigurator.Configure()

' Use Log4Net to log messages
Dim log As ILog = LogManager.GetLogger(GetType(Program))

Try
    ' Code that may throw exceptions
    Dim result As Double = 10 / 0
    Console.WriteLine($"Result: {result}")
Catch ex As DivideByZeroException
    ' Log the exception
    log.Error("Division by zero", ex)
Catch ex As Exception
    ' Log other exceptions
    log.Error("An error occurred", ex)
End Try
```

In this example, we configure Log4Net using an XML configuration file. We then create a logger instance and use it to log errors, including exceptions.

Error reporting involves collecting information about application errors and exceptions and transmitting that information to a central location for analysis and troubleshooting. Error reporting can take various forms, such as sending error reports via email, storing them in a database, or integrating with error tracking services like Sentry or Raygun.

Error reporting is particularly valuable in production environments, where it allows you to proactively address issues and improve the overall reliability of your application.

By implementing logging and error reporting effectively, you can gain insights into your application's behavior, detect and diagnose issues, and enhance the user experience by responding to errors promptly. These practices are essential for maintaining and supporting VB.NET applications in both development and production environments.

7.5 Best Practices in Error Handling

Effective error handling is crucial for building reliable and maintainable VB.NET applications. In this section, we'll discuss best practices and guidelines for error handling to ensure your code is robust and resilient.

1. Use Structured Exception Handling

VB.NET provides structured exception handling with Try, Catch, Finally, and Throw blocks. Always use structured exception handling to manage and handle exceptions, as it promotes clean and organized code.

```
Try
    ' Code that may throw exceptions
Catch ex As Exception
    ' Handle or log the exception
Finally
    ' Cleanup code (optional)
End Try
```

2. Be Specific in Exception Handling

Avoid using generic catch blocks that catch all exceptions unless you have a specific reason. Instead, catch only the exceptions you expect and can handle. This helps prevent unintended consequences and ensures you respond appropriately to different error scenarios.

```
Try
    ' Code that may throw specific exceptions
Catch ex As DivideByZeroException
    ' Handle division by zero error
Catch ex As ArgumentNullException
    ' Handle null argument error
End Try
```

3. Handle Exceptions at the Right Level

Handle exceptions at the appropriate level in your application. For example, catch and handle exceptions closest to where they occur to provide context-specific error messages to users. Higher-level exception handling can be used for logging and reporting.

4. Avoid Swallowing Exceptions

Avoid suppressing or swallowing exceptions without proper handling or logging. It can make debugging difficult and result in unnoticed issues. Log exceptions or rethrow them if necessary.

5. Implement Logging

As discussed earlier, implement a logging framework to record detailed information about exceptions and application behavior. Log exceptions, error messages, and relevant contextual information to aid in debugging and troubleshooting.

6. Provide User-Friendly Error Messages

When an exception occurs, display clear and user-friendly error messages whenever possible. Avoid exposing technical details to end-users, which can confuse or frustrate them. Log the technical details for debugging purposes.

7. Use Custom Exceptions

Create custom exceptions for specific error scenarios in your application. Custom exceptions can include additional information, making it easier to handle and diagnose errors. Use meaningful exception names for clarity.

8. Implement Error Reporting

In production environments, implement error reporting mechanisms to collect and analyze error data. Error reporting allows you to proactively identify and address issues, improving the reliability of your application.

9. Test Exception Handling

Thoroughly test your exception handling code. Include unit tests and simulate various error scenarios to ensure your code handles exceptions correctly. Testing helps uncover potential issues before they reach production.

10. Follow Best Practices in Finally Blocks

If you have cleanup code in a Finally block, ensure it does not throw exceptions, as it can mask the original exception. Keep Finally blocks simple and focused on cleanup tasks.

```
Try
    ' Code that may throw exceptions
Catch ex As Exception
    ' Handle the exception
Finally
    ' Clean up resources (without throwing exceptions)
End Try
```

11. Consider Global Exception Handling

For unhandled exceptions that may crash your application, consider implementing global exception handling at the application level. This can catch unexpected errors and provide a graceful way to handle them, such as displaying an error message and gracefully exiting the application.

```
AddHandler Application.ThreadException, AddressOf Application_ThreadException

Private Sub Application_ThreadException(sender As Object, e As Threading.Thre
adExceptionEventArgs)
    ' Handle unhandled exceptions here
    ' Log the exception and display an error message
End Sub
```

By following these best practices, you can build VB.NET applications that are more robust, maintainable, and user-friendly. Effective error handling is an essential part of creating software that meets user expectations and operates reliably in different scenarios.

Chapter 8: Multithreading and Asynchronous Programming

8.1 Introduction to Multithreading

Multithreading is a programming concept that enables a program to execute multiple threads concurrently, allowing it to perform multiple tasks in parallel. In this section, we'll introduce the fundamentals of multithreading in VB.NET and explore how it can improve the performance and responsiveness of your applications.

Understanding Threads

A thread is the smallest unit of execution in a program. In a single-threaded application, there is only one thread of execution, which means tasks are performed sequentially. In contrast, a multithreaded application can have multiple threads running simultaneously, each executing its own code independently.

Benefits of Multithreading

Multithreading offers several advantages, including:

1. **Improved Performance**: Multithreading can utilize multiple CPU cores, allowing tasks to execute concurrently and potentially speeding up CPU-bound operations.

2. **Responsiveness**: In user interfaces, multithreading can prevent the main thread from becoming unresponsive while performing time-consuming operations in the background.

3. **Parallelism**: Multithreading enables parallelism, making it suitable for tasks like data processing, rendering, and handling multiple client requests in server applications.

4. **Resource Utilization**: It can better utilize system resources, such as CPU and memory, by efficiently distributing tasks among threads.

Creating and Managing Threads

In VB.NET, you can create and manage threads using the `System.Threading` namespace. Here's a basic example of creating and starting a new thread:

```vb
Imports System.Threading

Sub Main()
    ' Create a new thread and specify the method to execute
    Dim thread As New Thread(AddressOf WorkerMethod)

    ' Start the thread
    thread.Start()
```

```vbnet
    ' Main thread continues executing here
    Console.WriteLine("Main thread is running.")

    ' Wait for the worker thread to finish
    thread.Join()

    Console.WriteLine("Main thread finished.")
End Sub

Sub WorkerMethod()
    Console.WriteLine("Worker thread is running.")
    ' Perform some work here
    Thread.Sleep(1000) ' Simulate work for 1 second
    Console.WriteLine("Worker thread finished.")
End Sub
```

In this example, we create a new thread using Thread, specify the method to execute (WorkerMethod), and start the thread using Start(). The main thread continues executing other code and waits for the worker thread to finish using Join().

Thread Synchronization

When multiple threads access shared data or resources, you need to ensure thread safety. Thread synchronization mechanisms like locks, mutexes, and semaphores are used to prevent data corruption and race conditions.

Challenges of Multithreading

While multithreading offers many advantages, it also introduces complexities such as synchronization issues, deadlocks, and increased debugging difficulty. It's important to carefully design and test multithreaded code to avoid these challenges.

In the subsequent sections of this chapter, we'll delve deeper into multithreading concepts, synchronization techniques, asynchronous programming with Async and Await, and parallel programming in VB.NET, allowing you to harness the power of concurrent execution in your applications.

8.2 Creating and Managing Threads

In the previous section, we introduced the fundamentals of multithreading in VB.NET. Now, let's explore how to create and manage threads in more detail. Thread management is crucial for building robust multithreaded applications.

Creating Threads

In VB.NET, you can create threads using the System.Threading.Thread class. To create a thread, follow these steps:

1. Define a method that represents the work you want the thread to perform.
2. Create a new instance of the Thread class, passing the method as a delegate to its constructor.
3. Start the thread using the Start() method.

Here's an example:

```
Imports System.Threading

Sub Main()
    ' Create a new thread and specify the method to execute
    Dim thread As New Thread(AddressOf WorkerMethod)

    ' Start the thread
    thread.Start()

    ' Main thread continues executing here
    Console.WriteLine("Main thread is running.")

    ' Wait for the worker thread to finish
    thread.Join()

    Console.WriteLine("Main thread finished.")
End Sub

Sub WorkerMethod()
    Console.WriteLine("Worker thread is running.")
    ' Perform some work here
    Thread.Sleep(1000) ' Simulate work for 1 second
    Console.WriteLine("Worker thread finished.")
End Sub
```

In this example, we create a new thread by instantiating the Thread class and specifying the WorkerMethod as the method to execute. Then, we start the thread with Start(). The main thread continues executing other code and waits for the worker thread to finish using Join().

Thread States

Threads can be in different states during their lifecycle:

- **Unstarted**: The thread is created but hasn't started yet.
- **Running**: The thread is actively executing.
- **Blocked**: The thread is waiting for an event, lock, or resource.
- **Dead**: The thread has finished executing.

You can query the state of a thread using its ThreadState property.

Thread Priorities

Threads can have different priorities, which affect how the operating system schedules them for execution. The priority range is typically from `ThreadPriority.Lowest` to `ThreadPriority.Highest`. Higher-priority threads get more CPU time.

```vbnet
Dim thread As New Thread(AddressOf WorkerMethod)
thread.Priority = ThreadPriority.AboveNormal ' Set thread priority
```

Thread Safety

When multiple threads access shared data or resources, thread safety becomes a concern. Synchronization mechanisms like locks (`SyncLock`), mutexes, and semaphores are used to protect shared resources and prevent data corruption.

```vbnet
Dim sharedData As Integer
Dim lockObject As New Object()

Sub UpdateSharedData()
    SyncLock lockObject
        sharedData += 1
    End SyncLock
End Sub
```

Thread Pooling

Creating a new thread for each task can be resource-intensive. VB.NET provides a thread pool (`ThreadPool`) to manage and reuse threads efficiently. It's suitable for short-lived tasks.

```vbnet
ThreadPool.QueueUserWorkItem(Sub(state) WorkerMethod())
```

The thread pool automatically manages the number of threads and assigns tasks to available threads.

In this section, we've explored how to create and manage threads in VB.NET, including thread states, priorities, and thread safety. Understanding thread management is essential for building responsive and scalable multithreaded applications. In the next section, we'll dive into synchronization and thread safety in more detail.

8.3 Synchronization and Thread Safety

In multithreaded applications, when multiple threads access shared data or resources concurrently, it's essential to ensure thread safety. Without proper synchronization, race conditions and data corruption can occur. In this section, we'll explore synchronization mechanisms and techniques to make your multithreaded VB.NET applications robust and safe.

Using Locks for Synchronization

One of the most common synchronization mechanisms in VB.NET is the `SyncLock` statement. It allows you to create a mutually exclusive block of code, ensuring that only one thread can execute it at a time. Here's an example:

```
Dim sharedData As Integer
Dim lockObject As New Object()

Sub UpdateSharedData()
    SyncLock lockObject
        sharedData += 1
    End SyncLock
End Sub
```

In this example, the `SyncLock` statement ensures that only one thread can increment the `sharedData` variable at a time, preventing data corruption.

Avoiding Deadlocks

Deadlocks occur when two or more threads are waiting for each other to release a resource, causing a standstill. To avoid deadlocks, follow these guidelines:

1. **Lock Resources in a Consistent Order**: Ensure that all threads lock resources in the same order to prevent circular waits.

2. **Use Timeout and Retry Strategies**: Implement timeouts and retry mechanisms to break deadlocks gracefully.

3. **Avoid Nested Locks**: Minimize the use of nested `SyncLock` statements, as they increase the risk of deadlocks.

Volatile Keyword for Shared Variables

When multiple threads read and write shared variables, you should use the `Volatile` keyword to ensure that the most up-to-date value is used. This keyword prevents the compiler from optimizing access to the variable. For example:

```
Dim sharedValue As Integer
Dim isRunning As Boolean

' Reading sharedValue
Dim value = Volatile.Read(sharedValue)

' Writing isRunning
Volatile.Write(isRunning, True)
```

Thread-Safe Collections

VB.NET provides thread-safe collections in the `System.Collections.Concurrent` namespace. These collections, such as ConcurrentQueue and `ConcurrentDictionary`, are designed for multithreaded access and eliminate the need for explicit locking.

```
Imports System.Collections.Concurrent

Dim queue As New ConcurrentQueue(Of Integer)()
queue.Enqueue(42)
Dim success As Boolean = queue.TryDequeue(value)
```

Atomic Operations

Some operations, such as incrementing or decrementing variables, can be made atomic using the `Interlocked` class. Atomic operations are thread-safe and don't require explicit synchronization.

```
Imports System.Threading

Dim counter As Integer

' Atomic increment
Interlocked.Increment(counter)

' Atomic decrement
Interlocked.Decrement(counter)
```

Immutable Data

Immutable data structures are inherently thread-safe because their state cannot be modified once created. When designing your classes, consider using immutability to simplify multithreading.

In this section, we've covered synchronization mechanisms like `SyncLock`, avoiding deadlocks, the `Volatile` keyword, thread-safe collections, atomic operations, and the concept of immutable data structures. These techniques are essential for building safe and efficient multithreaded VB.NET applications. In the next section, we'll delve into asynchronous programming with `Async` and `Await`.

8.4 Asynchronous Programming with Async/Await

Asynchronous programming is essential for building responsive and scalable applications. It allows your application to continue executing other tasks while waiting for time-consuming operations, such as I/O or network requests, to complete. VB.NET provides the `Async` and `Await` keywords to simplify asynchronous programming.

Understanding Asynchronous Programming

In traditional synchronous programming, a method blocks until a task is complete. This can lead to unresponsive applications when performing long-running operations. Asynchronous programming solves this problem by allowing a method to yield control to the calling thread while it awaits the completion of a task.

Using the Async and Await Keywords

To mark a method as asynchronous, use the Async keyword in its declaration. Inside the method, you can use the Await keyword before a task to indicate where the method should yield control. Here's an example of an asynchronous method that downloads a web page:

```
Imports System.Net.Http

Async Function DownloadWebPageAsync(url As String) As Task(Of String)
    Using client As New HttpClient()
        Dim response As HttpResponseMessage = Await client.GetAsync(url)
        Return Await response.Content.ReadAsStringAsync()
    End Using
End Function
```

In this example, the Await keyword is used before client.GetAsync() and response.Content.ReadAsStringAsync(), allowing the method to yield control back to the calling thread while waiting for the HTTP request and response processing.

Benefits of Asynchronous Programming

Asynchronous programming offers several benefits:

1. **Responsiveness**: Your application remains responsive to user input while performing background tasks.

2. **Scalability**: You can efficiently handle many concurrent operations without blocking threads.

3. **Resource Efficiency**: Asynchronous code reduces the need for thread creation and context switching, improving resource usage.

Exception Handling

When working with asynchronous code, it's crucial to handle exceptions correctly. You can use a Try...Catch block to handle exceptions that occur during asynchronous operations.

```
Try
    Dim result = Await DownloadWebPageAsync("https://example.com")
    Console.WriteLine(result)
Catch ex As Exception
    Console.WriteLine($"An error occurred: {ex.Message}")
End Try
```

Task and Task(Of T)

Asynchronous methods in VB.NET return instances of the `Task` or `Task(Of T)` class, representing ongoing or completed asynchronous operations. You can use these tasks to monitor the progress and completion of asynchronous operations.

Async/Await Best Practices

Here are some best practices for working with `Async` and `Await`:

1. **Avoid Async Void**: Prefer using `Async Function` over `Async Sub`. Async methods returning `Task` or `Task(Of T)` allow for better error handling and awaitability.

2. **Use ConfigureAwait**: When awaiting tasks, consider using `ConfigureAwait(False)` to prevent deadlocks in UI applications.

3. **Avoid Mixing Synchronous and Asynchronous Code**: Avoid blocking on asynchronous code with `.Result` or `.Wait()`, as it can lead to deadlocks.

4. **Error Handling**: Handle exceptions gracefully within asynchronous methods and log them appropriately.

In this section, we've explored asynchronous programming with the `Async` and `Await` keywords in VB.NET. These features are crucial for building responsive and scalable applications that can efficiently handle concurrent tasks. In the next section, we'll delve into parallel programming and how to leverage multiple cores for improved performance.

8.5 Parallel Programming in VB.NET

Parallel programming is the practice of breaking down tasks into smaller subtasks and executing them concurrently on multiple processing cores or threads. VB.NET provides several mechanisms for parallel programming, allowing you to harness the full potential of modern multi-core processors.

Parallel.ForEach and Parallel.For

The `Parallel.ForEach` and `Parallel.For` methods are powerful constructs for parallelizing loop iterations. They distribute the workload across available CPU cores, improving the efficiency of CPU-bound operations. Here's an example of using `Parallel.ForEach`:

```
Dim numbers As New List(Of Integer) From {1, 2, 3, 4, 5, 6, 7, 8, 9, 10}

Parallel.ForEach(numbers, Sub(number)
                    ' Perform parallel processing on 'number'
                    Console.WriteLine($"Processed {number}")
                End Sub)
```

In this example, each number is processed concurrently, and the order of processing may vary.

Task Parallel Library (TPL)

The Task Parallel Library (TPL) in .NET simplifies parallel programming by providing the Task class, which represents a unit of work. You can create and manage tasks to run operations in parallel. Here's an example:

```
Dim task1 As Task = Task.Run(Sub()
                        ' Perform parallel operation
                        Console.WriteLine("Task 1")
                    End Sub)

Dim task2 As Task = Task.Run(Sub()
                        ' Perform parallel operation
                        Console.WriteLine("Task 2")
                    End Sub)

Task.WaitAll(task1, task2)
```

In this example, Task.Run is used to execute two tasks concurrently, and Task.WaitAll ensures they both complete before proceeding.

PLINQ (Parallel LINQ)

PLINQ extends LINQ (Language Integrated Query) to support parallel execution of queries. It's especially useful for processing large datasets in parallel. Here's an example of using PLINQ to find even numbers:

```
Dim numbers As New List(Of Integer) From {1, 2, 3, 4, 5, 6, 7, 8, 9, 10}
Dim evenNumbers = numbers.AsParallel().Where(Function(n) n Mod 2 = 0)
```

PLINQ automatically parallelizes the filtering operation, optimizing performance for large collections.

Parallelism and Concurrency

It's important to understand the distinction between parallelism and concurrency. Parallelism involves executing multiple tasks simultaneously, typically for performance improvement. Concurrency, on the other hand, deals with managing multiple tasks that may overlap in time, such as in multi-threaded applications.

Thread Safety and Synchronization

When working with parallel programming, thread safety and synchronization become critical. Accessing shared data concurrently can lead to race conditions and data corruption. Use synchronization mechanisms like locks (SyncLock), monitors, and concurrent data structures to ensure thread safety.

Parallelism in Modern Applications

Parallel programming is especially valuable in modern applications that require processing large datasets, handling numerous client requests, or performing computationally intensive tasks. Leveraging multiple CPU cores can significantly improve application performance and responsiveness.

In this section, we've explored parallel programming in VB.NET, including `Parallel.ForEach`, `Parallel.For`, the Task Parallel Library (TPL), PLINQ, and the importance of thread safety and synchronization. These techniques are essential for harnessing the power of multi-core processors and building high-performance applications.

Chapter 9: Networking and Web Development with VB.NET

9.1 Building Web Applications with ASP.NET

ASP.NET is a powerful framework for building web applications in VB.NET. It provides a robust and flexible environment for creating dynamic, data-driven websites and web services. In this section, we'll explore the fundamentals of building web applications with ASP.NET.

Introduction to ASP.NET

ASP.NET is a part of the .NET framework designed for web development. It allows you to build web applications using a variety of languages, including VB.NET. ASP.NET offers two major programming models: Web Forms and ASP.NET MVC (Model-View-Controller).

Web Forms

Web Forms is a component-based framework that simplifies web application development. It provides a drag-and-drop visual designer, making it easy to create user interfaces. You can write event-driven code to handle user interactions, making it suitable for rapid application development (RAD).

ASP.NET MVC

ASP.NET MVC is a framework that follows the Model-View-Controller architectural pattern. It emphasizes separation of concerns and provides full control over HTML markup. MVC is well-suited for complex web applications and RESTful services.

Creating an ASP.NET Web Application

To create an ASP.NET web application in Visual Studio, follow these steps:

1. Open Visual Studio.

2. Go to "File" > "New" > "Project."

3. Select "ASP.NET Web Application" as the project template.

4. Choose a project name and location.

5. Click "Create."

Web Forms vs. MVC

When creating an ASP.NET web application, you'll need to choose between Web Forms and MVC. Consider the following factors:

- **Complexity**: If you need full control over HTML and CSS, and your application has complex requirements, MVC might be a better choice.

- **Rapid Development**: For quick prototyping and development, Web Forms with its visual designer can be more productive.

- **Maintenance**: MVC enforces separation of concerns, making it easier to maintain and test your application over time.

In ASP.NET Web Forms, you can create a simple web page by designing it in the visual designer. You can drag and drop controls like buttons, textboxes, and labels onto the page. Then, you can write event handlers in VB.NET to respond to user actions.

Here's an example of a simple ASP.NET web page with a button and label:

```
<%@ Page Language="VB" AutoEventWireup="true" CodeBehind="WebForm1.aspx.vb" I
nherits="WebApplication1.WebForm1" %>

<!DOCTYPE html>

<html xmlns="http://www.w3.org/1999/xhtml">
<head runat="server">
    <title>ASP.NET Web Page</title>
</head>
<body>
    <form id="form1" runat="server">
        <asp:Button ID="btnClickMe" runat="server" Text="Click Me" OnClick="b
tnClickMe_Click" />
        <br />
        <asp:Label ID="lblMessage" runat="server" Text=""></asp:Label>
    </form>
</body>
</html>
```

In the code-behind file (WebForm1.aspx.vb), you can write the event handler for the button click:

```
Partial Class WebForm1
    Inherits System.Web.UI.Page

    Protected Sub btnClickMe_Click(sender As Object, e As EventArgs) Handles
btnClickMe.Click
        lblMessage.Text = "Hello, ASP.NET Web Forms!"
    End Sub
End Class
```

This code displays a message when the button is clicked.

ASP.NET is a versatile framework for building web applications in VB.NET. Whether you choose Web Forms or MVC depends on your project's requirements. In the next sections, we'll dive deeper into web development with ASP.NET, covering topics like data access, web services, and real-time communication.

9.2 Web Forms and MVC Frameworks

In the realm of web development with VB.NET, two primary frameworks are often utilized: Web Forms and ASP.NET MVC (Model-View-Controller). Each framework has distinct characteristics and use cases, making them suitable for different types of web applications. In this section, we'll delve into the key features and considerations for both frameworks.

Web Forms

Web Forms is a component-based framework that simplifies web application development through a visual design surface. It follows a stateful model, where the server retains control state, allowing you to create interactive and event-driven web applications rapidly.

Key features of Web Forms include:

- **Drag-and-Drop Design**: The Visual Studio IDE offers a drag-and-drop interface for designing web pages, making it easy to create user interfaces.

- **Event-Driven Programming**: You can write code-behind files in VB.NET to handle events generated by user interactions, such as button clicks.

- **Server Controls**: Web Forms provides a wide range of server controls, like buttons, textboxes, and grids, which encapsulate complex HTML and JavaScript behavior.

- **ViewState**: ViewState allows Web Forms to maintain the state of controls across postbacks, simplifying user interface development.

Web Forms is well-suited for applications requiring rapid development, especially when you need to create data-driven web interfaces quickly. However, its postback mechanism can lead to larger view states and potentially affect performance in very data-intensive applications.

ASP.NET MVC

ASP.NET MVC (Model-View-Controller) is a framework that promotes the separation of concerns and provides full control over HTML markup. It follows a stateless and RESTful approach to web development.

Key features of ASP.NET MVC include:

- **Separation of Concerns**: MVC enforces a clear separation between the model (data and business logic), view (user interface), and controller (request handling and logic). This separation makes the application more maintainable and testable.

- **Control Over Markup**: Developers have complete control over HTML markup, making it ideal for creating clean, semantically meaningful web pages.

- **Routing**: MVC uses routing to map URLs to controller actions, offering flexibility in defining URL structures.

- **Testability**: The separation of concerns in MVC makes it easier to write unit tests for different parts of the application.

ASP.NET MVC is a good choice for complex web applications where fine-grained control over HTML, CSS, and JavaScript is essential. It's also a popular choice for building RESTful APIs.

Choosing Between Web Forms and MVC

The choice between Web Forms and MVC depends on your project's requirements:

- **Web Forms** is suitable for:
    - Rapid application development (RAD).
    - Applications requiring complex, data-driven user interfaces.
    - Projects where you need to leverage the visual designer in Visual Studio.
- **MVC** is suitable for:
    - Applications with complex business logic.
    - Projects that demand fine control over HTML and CSS.
    - RESTful API development.
      Teams that prioritize testability and maintainability.

It's important to note that both frameworks can coexist in the same project. For example, you can use MVC for the core application logic and Web Forms for specific user interfaces or features.

In conclusion, both Web Forms and MVC are valuable frameworks for web development with VB.NET, each catering to different project requirements and development styles. Your choice should align with your project's objectives and the level of control and separation of concerns you require.

9.3 Consuming Web Services

In the world of modern web development, applications often need to interact with external services and APIs to access data or perform specific actions. VB.NET provides various mechanisms to consume web services, including RESTful APIs, SOAP services, and more. In this section, we'll explore how to consume web services in VB.NET.

Understanding Web Services

Web services are software components accessible over the internet using standard protocols. They allow applications to communicate and share data or functionality. Two common types of web services are:

- **RESTful Web Services**: REST (Representational State Transfer) is an architectural style for designing networked applications. RESTful APIs use HTTP methods (GET, POST, PUT, DELETE) to perform actions on resources identified by URLs.

- **SOAP Web Services**: SOAP (Simple Object Access Protocol) is a protocol for exchanging structured information in the implementation of web services. SOAP services often use XML for data exchange and can be accessed over HTTP, SMTP, or other transport protocols.

Consuming RESTful Web Services

Consuming RESTful APIs in VB.NET typically involves making HTTP requests and processing JSON or XML responses. You can use the HttpClient class in the System.Net.Http namespace for this purpose. Here's a basic example of consuming a RESTful API:

```
Imports System.Net.Http

Public Async Function GetWeatherAsync(city As String) As Task(Of String)
    Using client As New HttpClient()
        Dim response = Await client.GetAsync($"https://api.example.com/weathe
r?city={city}")
        If response.IsSuccessStatusCode Then
            Dim content = Await response.Content.ReadAsStringAsync()
            Return content
        Else
            Return $"Error: {response.StatusCode}"
        End If
    End Using
End Function
```

In this example, we define a function that sends an HTTP GET request to a weather API and returns the response content as a string. You can further parse the response to work with the data.

Consuming SOAP Web Services

Consuming SOAP web services in VB.NET often involves adding a service reference to your project. You provide the service's WSDL (Web Services Description Language) URL, and Visual Studio generates client proxy classes for you. Here's a high-level overview of the process:

1. Right-click on your project and select "Add Service Reference."

2. Enter the WSDL URL of the SOAP service you want to consume.

3. Visual Studio generates proxy classes that represent the service and its methods.

4. You can then use these proxy classes to interact with the service as if it were a local object.

Here's a simplified example of consuming a SOAP web service after adding a service reference:

```vb
Imports MyServiceReference ' Import the generated service reference namespace

Public Function GetUserInfo(userId As Integer) As UserInfo
    Using client As New MyServiceClient() ' Instantiate the client
        Return client.GetUserInfo(userId) ' Call the service method
    End Using
End Function
```

In this example, we import the service reference namespace and create an instance of the client proxy class (MyServiceClient). We can then call methods on this client to interact with the SOAP service.

Error Handling and Security

When consuming web services, it's essential to implement error handling to handle potential network issues, service unavailability, or unexpected responses. Additionally, consider security aspects, such as authentication and data encryption, when working with sensitive data over the internet.

In conclusion, VB.NET provides the tools and libraries necessary to consume various web services, whether they follow RESTful or SOAP-based architectures. Understanding the type of web service you're working with and leveraging the appropriate libraries and techniques is crucial for successful integration into your VB.NET applications.

9.4 Working with RESTful APIs

RESTful APIs (Representational State Transfer Application Programming Interfaces) have become a standard way to interact with web services due to their simplicity and scalability. In this section, we'll explore how to work with RESTful APIs in VB.NET.

Making HTTP Requests

To interact with a RESTful API, you'll need to make HTTP requests. VB.NET provides the HttpClient class in the System.Net.Http namespace for this purpose. Here's a basic example of making an HTTP GET request to retrieve data from a RESTful API:

```vb
Imports System.Net.Http
```

```vbnet
Public Async Function GetResourceAsync() As Task(Of String)
    Using client As New HttpClient()
        Dim response = Await client.GetAsync("https://api.example.com/resourc
e")

        If response.IsSuccessStatusCode Then
            Dim content = Await response.Content.ReadAsStringAsync()
            Return content
        Else
            Return $"Error: {response.StatusCode}"
        End If
    End Using
End Function
```

In this example, we create an `HttpClient` instance, send an HTTP GET request to a URL, and read the response content. You can adjust the URL and HTTP method according to the API's documentation.

Handling JSON Data

RESTful APIs often return data in JSON format. You can use libraries like `System.Text.Json` or Newtonsoft.Json (Json.NET) to parse JSON responses. Here's a simple example using `System.Text.Json`:

```vbnet
Imports System.Text.Json

Public Class MyData
    Public Property Name As String
    Public Property Age As Integer
End Class

Public Async Function ParseJsonAsync(jsonData As String) As Task(Of MyData)
    Dim options As New JsonSerializerOptions()
    options.PropertyNameCaseInsensitive = True
    Return JsonSerializer.Deserialize(Of MyData)(jsonData, options)
End Function
```

In this code, we define a class `MyData` that matches the structure of the JSON data we expect. We use `JsonSerializer.Deserialize` to convert the JSON string into a .NET object.

Sending Data

When interacting with RESTful APIs, you may need to send data, typically in the request body, for operations like creating or updating resources. Here's an example of sending JSON data in an HTTP POST request:

```vbnet
Imports System.Net.Http
Imports System.Text
Imports System.Text.Json

Public Async Function CreateResourceAsync(data As MyData) As Task(Of String)
```

```
    Using client As New HttpClient()
        Dim jsonData = JsonSerializer.Serialize(data)
        Dim content = New StringContent(jsonData, Encoding.UTF8, "application
/json")

        Dim response = Await client.PostAsync("https://api.example.com/resour
ce", content)

        If response.IsSuccessStatusCode Then
            Dim responseContent = Await response.Content.ReadAsStringAsync()
            Return responseContent
        Else
            Return $"Error: {response.StatusCode}"
        End If
    End Using
End Function
```

In this example, we serialize a MyData object to JSON and send it in the request body as
application/json content.

Authentication and Authorization

Many RESTful APIs require authentication or authorization. You can include authentication
tokens, API keys, or credentials in your HTTP requests as needed. Ensure that you follow
the API documentation for the correct authentication method.

Working with RESTful APIs in VB.NET is versatile and allows you to integrate your
applications with a wide range of web services and data sources. Be sure to review the API
documentation for specific requirements and best practices for each API you interact with.

9.5 Real-Time Communication with SignalR

Real-time communication is crucial in many modern web applications to provide live
updates, chat features, and interactive experiences. SignalR is a popular library in the .NET
ecosystem that enables real-time functionality. In this section, we'll explore how to use
SignalR for real-time communication in VB.NET applications.

What is SignalR?

SignalR is a library that simplifies real-time web communication between the server and
connected clients. It allows the server to push content to connected clients instantly,
eliminating the need for clients to poll the server for updates. SignalR works seamlessly
with ASP.NET Core, making it a great choice for building real-time features in web
applications.

To get started with SignalR in a VB.NET application, you'll need to set up an ASP.NET Core project or use an existing one. You can add SignalR to your project by installing the `Microsoft.AspNetCore.SignalR` NuGet package.

Once SignalR is added to your project, you can configure it in your Startup class. Here's an example of configuring SignalR in a `Startup.vb` file:

```vbnet
Imports Microsoft.AspNetCore.Builder
Imports Microsoft.Extensions.DependencyInjection

Public Class Startup
    Public Sub ConfigureServices(ByVal services As IServiceCollection)
        ' Other services configuration
        services.AddSignalR()
    End Sub

    Public Sub Configure(ByVal app As IApplicationBuilder)
        ' Other middleware configuration
        app.UseEndpoints(Sub(endpoints)
                            endpoints.MapHub(Of ChatHub)("/chatHub")
                        End Sub)
    End Sub
End Class
```

In this example, we add SignalR to the services and configure a hub endpoint for real-time communication.

Creating a SignalR Hub

A SignalR hub is a server-side class that handles real-time communication with clients. You can create a hub by inheriting from the Hub class. Here's an example of a simple chat hub:

```vbnet
Imports Microsoft.AspNetCore.SignalR

Public Class ChatHub
    Inherits Hub

    Public Async Function SendMessage(ByVal user As String, ByVal message As String) As Task
        Await Clients.All.SendAsync("ReceiveMessage", user, message)
    End Function
End Class
```

In this code, the `SendMessage` method sends a message to all connected clients.

To connect to SignalR from a VB.NET client, you can use the SignalR .NET client library. Install the `Microsoft.AspNetCore.SignalR.Client` NuGet package to your client application.

Here's a simple example of how a VB.NET client can connect to the SignalR hub and receive messages:

```vbnet
Imports Microsoft.AspNetCore.SignalR.Client

Module Program
    Public Async Function Main() As Task
        Dim connection As HubConnection = New HubConnectionBuilder() _
            .WithUrl("https://yourserverurl/chatHub") _
            .Build()

        AddHandler connection.On(Of String, String)("ReceiveMessage", Sub(user, message)
                                                                           Console.WriteLine($"{user}: {message}")
                                                                       End Sub)

        Await connection.StartAsync()

        Console.WriteLine("Connected to the chat.")
        Console.ReadLine()
    End Function
End Module
```

In this client code, we configure a connection to the SignalR hub and handle the ReceiveMessage event to display incoming messages.

Real-Time Features with SignalR

SignalR opens up various possibilities for real-time features in your VB.NET applications, such as chat applications, live notifications, collaborative editing, and more. You can customize your SignalR hub and client to meet the specific requirements of your application.

Remember to secure your SignalR communication and handle connection management and errors effectively for a robust real-time experience in your VB.NET projects.

Chapter 10: Working with Databases and ORM

10.1 Database Connectivity Options

In modern software development, databases play a crucial role in storing and retrieving data. VB.NET provides various options for connecting to databases, allowing you to work with relational databases, NoSQL databases, and object-relational mapping (ORM) frameworks. In this section, we'll explore the different database connectivity options available in VB.NET.

ADO.NET

ADO.NET (ActiveX Data Objects for .NET) is a core technology for database access in VB.NET. It provides a set of classes and libraries for connecting to and working with relational databases like Microsoft SQL Server, MySQL, and Oracle. ADO.NET uses a provider model, allowing you to use different database providers with the same codebase.

Here's a simplified example of connecting to a SQL Server database using ADO.NET:

```
Imports System.Data.SqlClient

Module Program
    Sub Main()
        Dim connectionString As String = "Data Source=ServerName;Initial Cata
log=DatabaseName;User ID=UserName;Password=Password"

        Using connection As New SqlConnection(connectionString)
            connection.Open()

            ' Perform database operations here

        End Using
    End Sub
End Module
```

ADO.NET provides various classes like `SqlConnection`, `SqlCommand`, and `SqlDataReader` to interact with the database, execute queries, and retrieve results.

Entity Framework (EF)

Entity Framework is a popular ORM framework for VB.NET that simplifies database access by allowing you to work with objects instead of writing raw SQL queries. EF provides a high-level abstraction over the database, making it easier to perform CRUD (Create, Read, Update, Delete) operations and work with database schema.

Here's an example of using Entity Framework to query data from a database:

```vbnet
Imports System.Data.Entity

Public Class Customer
    Public Property Id As Integer
    Public Property Name As String
End Class

Public Class CustomerDbContext
    Inherits DbContext
    Public Property Customers As DbSet(Of Customer)
End Class

Module Program
    Sub Main()
        Using context As New CustomerDbContext()
            Dim customers = context.Customers.ToList()

            For Each customer In customers
                Console.WriteLine($"Customer ID: {customer.Id}, Name: {custom
er.Name}")
            Next
        End Using
    End Sub
End Module
```

EF automatically generates SQL queries based on LINQ expressions, abstracting the underlying database details.

NoSQL Databases

In addition to relational databases, VB.NET supports working with NoSQL databases like MongoDB, Redis, and Couchbase. NoSQL databases are schema-less and are suitable for storing unstructured or semi-structured data. Libraries and drivers are available for VB.NET to connect to various NoSQL databases.

Here's an example of using the MongoDB driver for VB.NET to work with a MongoDB database:

```vbnet
Imports MongoDB.Driver

Module Program
    Sub Main()
        Dim client As New MongoClient("mongodb://localhost:27017")
        Dim database As IMongoDatabase = client.GetDatabase("mydb")
        Dim collection As IMongoCollection(Of BsonDocument) = database.GetCol
lection(Of BsonDocument)("mycollection")

        ' Perform MongoDB operations here
```

```
        End Sub
End Module
```

The choice of a database connectivity option in VB.NET depends on your project's requirements, existing infrastructure, and familiarity with the technology. ADO.NET is suitable for low-level database access, Entity Framework provides an ORM approach for relational databases, and NoSQL libraries are ideal for non-relational data stores.

When selecting a database connectivity option, consider factors like data volume, performance, scalability, and ease of development. Additionally, ensure that you follow best practices for database access to maintain data integrity and security in your VB.NET applications.

10.2 Entity Framework and ORM Concepts

Entity Framework (EF) is a powerful Object-Relational Mapping (ORM) framework for VB.NET and other .NET languages. It simplifies database interaction by allowing developers to work with objects in their applications rather than writing SQL queries. In this section, we will delve into the core concepts of Entity Framework and how it enables ORM in VB.NET applications.

Entities and DbContext

In Entity Framework, an entity represents a class that corresponds to a database table. Each property of the entity class typically maps to a column in the table. For example, consider an entity for a "Product" table:

```
Public Class Product
    Public Property ProductId As Integer
    Public Property Name As String
    Public Property Price As Decimal
End Class
```

The Product class represents the "Product" table in the database. The properties ProductId, Name, and Price map to the corresponding columns.

The DbContext class serves as the entry point to the Entity Framework and represents a session with the database. It is responsible for managing database connections and providing access to entities. Here's an example of a simple DbContext:

```
Imports System.Data.Entity

Public Class ProductDbContext
    Inherits DbContext
```

```
    Public Property Products As DbSet(Of Product)
End Class
```

In this example, the `ProductDbContext` class exposes a `DbSet` property for the `Product` entity. It indicates that Entity Framework should track and manage `Product` entities in the database.

CRUD Operations with Entity Framework

Entity Framework simplifies CRUD (Create, Read, Update, Delete) operations. Here's how you can perform these operations with Entity Framework:

Create (Insert) a New Entity

To add a new entity to the database, create an instance of the entity class and add it to the `DbSet`. Entity Framework will automatically track the changes and insert the entity into the database when you call `SaveChanges` on the `DbContext`.

```
Using context As New ProductDbContext()
    Dim newProduct As New Product() With {
        .Name = "New Product",
        .Price = 19.99
    }

    context.Products.Add(newProduct)
    context.SaveChanges()
End Using
```

Read (Query) Data

Entity Framework allows you to query data using LINQ (Language Integrated Query) expressions. Here's an example of querying products with a specific price:

```
Using context As New ProductDbContext()
    Dim affordableProducts = From p In context.Products
                             Where p.Price < 20.0
                             Select p

    For Each product In affordableProducts
        Console.WriteLine($"Product ID: {product.ProductId}, Name: {product.N
ame}, Price: {product.Price}")
    Next
End Using
```

Update an Entity

Updating an entity involves querying for the entity, modifying its properties, and then calling `SaveChanges` to persist the changes to the database.

```
Using context As New ProductDbContext()
    Dim productToUpdate = context.Products.Find(1) ' Assuming product with ID
```

```
1 exists
    If productToUpdate IsNot Nothing Then
        productToUpdate.Name = "Updated Product Name"
        context.SaveChanges()
    End If
End Using
```

Delete an Entity

To delete an entity, you can retrieve it and then remove it from the DbSet before calling SaveChanges.

```
Using context As New ProductDbContext()
    Dim productToDelete = context.Products.Find(1) ' Assuming product with ID
1 exists
    If productToDelete IsNot Nothing Then
        context.Products.Remove(productToDelete)
        context.SaveChanges()
    End If
End Using
```

Automatic Migration

Entity Framework includes a feature called Automatic Migrations, which simplifies database schema changes. When you modify your entity classes or DbContext, Entity Framework can automatically generate the SQL scripts necessary to update the database schema to match the changes in your code.

Summary

Entity Framework is a powerful ORM framework that simplifies database interactions in VB.NET applications. It allows you to work with entities, provides a DbContext for database access, and supports CRUD operations using LINQ queries. Additionally, it offers features like Automatic Migrations for managing database schema changes. By understanding these fundamental concepts, you can leverage Entity Framework to efficiently work with databases in your VB.NET projects.

10.3 Querying and Manipulating Data

In the previous section, we discussed the basics of Entity Framework and how to perform CRUD operations. Now, let's dive deeper into querying and manipulating data using Entity Framework in VB.NET.

Querying Data

Entity Framework allows you to query data from the database using LINQ (Language Integrated Query) expressions. This provides a powerful and expressive way to retrieve data.

Here's an example of querying all products with a price less than $50:

```
Using context As New ProductDbContext()
    Dim affordableProducts = From p In context.Products
                             Where p.Price < 50.0
                             Select p

    For Each product In affordableProducts
        Console.WriteLine($"Product ID: {product.ProductId}, Name: {product.N
ame}, Price: {product.Price}")
    Next
End Using
```

Eager Loading

Entity Framework supports eager loading, which allows you to load related entities along with the main entity to minimize database round trips. For example, if you have a Product entity with a navigation property Category, you can eagerly load the category:

```
Using context As New ProductDbContext()
    Dim productsWithCategories = context.Products.Include(Function(p) p.Categ
ory).ToList()

    For Each product In productsWithCategories
        Console.WriteLine($"Product ID: {product.ProductId}, Name: {product.N
ame}, Category: {product.Category.Name}")
    Next
End Using
```

Manipulating Data

Entity Framework provides various ways to manipulate data, including adding, updating, and deleting records.

Adding Data

To add a new record to the database, create an instance of the entity class, add it to the DbSet, and call SaveChanges.

```
Using context As New ProductDbContext()
    Dim newProduct As New Product() With {
        .Name = "New Product",
        .Price = 19.99
    }

    context.Products.Add(newProduct)
    context.SaveChanges()
End Using
```

To update an existing record, query for the entity, modify its properties, and call SaveChanges to persist the changes.

```
Using context As New ProductDbContext()
    Dim productToUpdate = context.Products.Find(1) ' Assuming product with ID
1 exists
    If productToUpdate IsNot Nothing Then
        productToUpdate.Name = "Updated Product Name"
        context.SaveChanges()
    End If
End Using
```

Deleting Data

To delete a record, retrieve it from the DbSet, remove it, and call SaveChanges.

```
Using context As New ProductDbContext()
    Dim productToDelete = context.Products.Find(1) ' Assuming product with ID
1 exists
    If productToDelete IsNot Nothing Then
        context.Products.Remove(productToDelete)
        context.SaveChanges()
    End If
End Using
```

Transactions

Entity Framework supports transactions, allowing you to group multiple database operations into a single transaction. This ensures that either all operations are completed successfully or none of them are.

```
Using context As New ProductDbContext()
    Using transaction = context.Database.BeginTransaction()
        Try
            ' Perform database operations here
            context.SaveChanges()
            transaction.Commit()
        Catch ex As Exception
            transaction.Rollback()
            ' Handle the exception
        End Try
    End Using
End Using
```

Summary

Entity Framework in VB.NET simplifies data querying and manipulation with its support for LINQ, eager loading, and transaction management. By understanding these concepts, you can efficiently work with databases in your VB.NET applications while maintaining code readability and flexibility.

10.4 Advanced Database Topics

In this section, we will explore advanced database topics related to Entity Framework in VB.NET. These topics cover more advanced scenarios and techniques that can help you work effectively with databases in your applications.

1. Transactions

Transactions are a crucial aspect of working with databases, ensuring the consistency and integrity of data. Entity Framework supports transactions, allowing you to perform multiple operations as a single unit of work. This is particularly useful when you need to ensure that a series of operations either succeed together or fail together.

Here's an example of how to use transactions in Entity Framework:

```vbnet
Using context As New ProductDbContext()
    Using transaction = context.Database.BeginTransaction()
        Try
            ' Perform multiple database operations here
            context.SaveChanges()
            transaction.Commit()
        Catch ex As Exception
            transaction.Rollback()
            ' Handle the exception
        End Try
    End Using
End Using
```

2. Stored Procedures

Entity Framework can work with stored procedures defined in your database. You can call stored procedures and map their results to entities or complex types. This is useful for scenarios where you have complex business logic in the database or want to leverage existing stored procedures.

```vbnet
Using context As New ProductDbContext()
    Dim categoryId As Integer = 1
    Dim products = context.Database.SqlQuery(Of Product)("EXEC GetProductsByC
ategory @categoryId", New SqlParameter("@categoryId", categoryId)).ToList()
End Using
```

3. Code-First Migrations

Code-First Migrations allow you to evolve your database schema as your application evolves. You can define changes to your database schema using code-first conventions, and Entity Framework will generate SQL scripts to apply these changes.

To enable migrations, use the Package Manager Console:

```
Enable-Migrations
```

Then, you can create a migration and update the database:

```
Add-Migration InitialCreate
Update-Database
```

4. Database Seeding

Database seeding is the process of populating your database with initial data. Entity Framework supports database seeding through the DbSet.Seed() method. You can use this method to add initial records when the database is created.

```
Protected Overrides Sub Seed(context As ProductDbContext)
    context.Products.AddOrUpdate(
        Function(p) p.Name,
        New Product() With {.Name = "Product1", .Price = 19.99},
        New Product() With {.Name = "Product2", .Price = 29.99}
    )
End Sub
```

5. Database Views

Entity Framework can map database views to entities, allowing you to work with views just like tables. This is helpful when you want to encapsulate complex queries as views and access them through Entity Framework.

```
Public Class ProductView
    Public Property ProductId As Integer
    Public Property Name As String
    Public Property CategoryName As String
End Class

Using context As New ProductDbContext()
    Dim productViews = context.ProductViews.ToList()
End Using
```

6. Database Interception

Entity Framework provides interception points to inspect and modify database commands before they are executed. You can use this feature for logging, performance monitoring, or customizing queries.

```vbnet
Public Class MyInterceptor
    Implements IDbCommandInterceptor

    Public Sub NonQueryExecuting(command As DbCommand, interceptionContext As
DbCommandInterceptionContext(Of Integer)) Implements IDbCommandInterceptor.No
nQueryExecuting
        ' Modify or log the command here
    End Sub

    ' Implement other interceptor methods as needed
End Class

' Register the interceptor
DbInterception.Add(New MyInterceptor())
```

These advanced topics expand your capabilities when working with Entity Framework and databases in VB.NET. Understanding transactions, stored procedures, migrations, seeding, views, and interception can help you tackle complex database-related challenges in your applications.

10.5 NoSQL Databases and VB.NET

In this section, we'll explore the integration of VB.NET with NoSQL databases. While VB.NET has traditionally been associated with relational databases, NoSQL databases provide a different approach to data storage, focusing on flexibility and scalability. We'll discuss what NoSQL databases are, how to work with them in VB.NET, and scenarios where they are a suitable choice.

What Are NoSQL Databases?

NoSQL databases, often referred to as "Not Only SQL," are a class of databases that differ from traditional relational databases in their data models. Unlike relational databases, which use structured schemas and tables, NoSQL databases are schema-less or have flexible schemas. They are designed to handle large volumes of unstructured or semi-structured data and offer horizontal scalability.

There are several types of NoSQL databases, including:

1. **Document Databases:** These databases store data in documents, typically in JSON or BSON format. Each document can have a different structure, making them suitable for semi-structured data. Examples include MongoDB and Couchbase.

2. **Key-Value Stores:** Key-value stores store data as key-value pairs. They are highly efficient for simple read and write operations. Examples include Redis and Amazon DynamoDB.

3. **Column-Family Stores:** These databases store data in column families rather than tables. They are designed for high write throughput. Examples include Apache Cassandra and HBase.

4. **Graph Databases:** Graph databases are used to store and query data with complex relationships. They are suitable for applications like social networks and recommendation systems. Examples include Neo4j and Amazon Neptune.

Working with NoSQL Databases in VB.NET

Integrating VB.NET with NoSQL databases involves using appropriate libraries or drivers provided by the database vendors. Here's an example of working with a document database like MongoDB in VB.NET:

```
Imports MongoDB.Bson
Imports MongoDB.Driver

' Connect to MongoDB
Dim client As New MongoClient("mongodb://localhost:27017")
Dim database As IMongoDatabase = client.GetDatabase("mydb")
Dim collection As IMongoCollection(Of BsonDocument) = database.GetCollection(
Of BsonDocument)("mycollection")

' Insert a document
Dim document As New BsonDocument()
document.Add("name", "John")
document.Add("age", 30)
collection.InsertOne(document)

' Query documents
Dim filter = Builders(Of BsonDocument).Filter.Eq("name", "John")
Dim result = collection.Find(filter).ToList()
```

For key-value stores like Redis, you can use libraries like StackExchange.Redis to interact with the database.

When to Use NoSQL Databases

NoSQL databases are suitable for various scenarios, including:

- **Handling Large Amounts of Data:** NoSQL databases excel at handling large volumes of data, making them a good choice for applications with scalability requirements.

- **Unstructured or Semi-Structured Data:** If your data doesn't fit neatly into a tabular structure, NoSQL databases can accommodate flexible data models.

- **Rapid Development:** NoSQL databases are often chosen for their ease of development and adaptability to changing requirements.

- **Real-Time Analytics:** NoSQL databases can support real-time analytics and event-driven architectures.

However, it's essential to choose the right database type within the NoSQL category that aligns with your specific use case. Relational databases are still a strong choice for applications that require complex querying, ACID transactions, and strong data consistency.

In conclusion, NoSQL databases provide an alternative to traditional relational databases, offering flexibility and scalability. VB.NET developers can work with NoSQL databases by using appropriate libraries or drivers, depending on the database type. Understanding the strengths and limitations of NoSQL databases is essential for making informed architectural decisions in your VB.NET projects.

Chapter 11: Windows Desktop Application Development

Section 11.1: Developing Desktop Applications

In this section, we will explore the development of Windows desktop applications using Visual Basic .NET (VB.NET). Windows desktop applications are traditional software programs designed to run on Microsoft Windows operating systems. They provide a graphical user interface (GUI) that allows users to interact with the application using windows, dialogs, buttons, and other graphical elements.

Windows Forms Applications

One of the primary ways to create Windows desktop applications in VB.NET is by using Windows Forms (WinForms). Windows Forms is a graphical user interface library that provides a set of classes and controls for building rich desktop applications. These applications can range from simple utility tools to complex business applications.

Creating a Windows Forms application typically involves the following steps:

1. **Create a New Windows Forms Project:** You can start by creating a new Windows Forms project in your integrated development environment (IDE) such as Visual Studio. This sets up the basic project structure and form designer.

2. **Design User Interfaces:** Use the form designer to design the user interfaces of your application. You can drag and drop controls like buttons, text boxes, labels, and more onto your forms. Then, you can customize their properties and layout.

3. **Write Code-Behind:** VB.NET allows you to write code-behind for your forms. This code defines the behavior and functionality of your application. You can handle events like button clicks, form load, and user input to create responsive applications.

4. **Build and Debug:** Once you've designed your forms and written the code-behind, you can build and debug your application. The IDE provides debugging tools to help you identify and fix issues.

5. **Deployment:** After successful development and testing, you can deploy your Windows Forms application to other Windows machines. This typically involves creating an installer that packages your application for distribution.

Advantages of Windows Desktop Applications

Windows desktop applications offer several advantages:

- **Rich User Experience:** They provide a rich and responsive user interface, making them suitable for applications that require complex interactions.

- **Access to Local Resources:** Desktop applications have access to local system resources such as file systems, printers, and hardware peripherals.

- **Offline Functionality:** Users can run desktop applications even when they are not connected to the internet.

- **Customizability:** Developers have full control over the look and feel of the application's GUI.

- **Performance:** Desktop applications can take advantage of the full processing power of the user's machine, leading to better performance for resource-intensive tasks.

In the upcoming sections of this chapter, we will delve deeper into various aspects of Windows desktop application development, including advanced WinForms features, integrating Windows Presentation Foundation (WPF), building Windows services, and strategies for deployment and distribution.

Section 11.2: Advanced WinForms Features

In this section, we will explore advanced features and techniques for Windows Forms (WinForms) application development in Visual Basic .NET (VB.NET). Building upon the basics introduced in Section 11.1, we'll delve into more complex aspects of WinForms to create powerful and feature-rich desktop applications.

Custom Controls

WinForms allows you to create custom controls that extend the functionality of the standard controls provided by the framework. Custom controls are reusable components that encapsulate specific behaviors or user interface elements. You can design and implement custom controls to suit the unique requirements of your application.

Creating custom controls involves:

1. **Inheritance:** You typically inherit from an existing WinForms control, such as Control or UserControl, to create your custom control.

2. **Custom Painting:** You can override the OnPaint method to customize how your control is drawn on the screen. This allows you to create visually distinct controls.

3. **Properties and Events:** Define properties and events for your custom control to make it configurable and interactive. This allows developers who use your control to customize its behavior.

4. **Design-Time Support:** Implement design-time support so that your custom control can be easily added and configured in the Visual Studio form designer.

Data Binding

Data binding is a powerful feature in WinForms that allows you to connect the user interface of your application directly to data sources such as databases, collections, or objects. This simplifies the process of displaying and editing data in your application's forms.

Key concepts related to data binding in WinForms include:

- **BindingSource:** The BindingSource component acts as an intermediary between your data source and WinForms controls. It simplifies data binding and provides features like sorting and filtering.

- **Data Binding Expressions:** You can use data binding expressions to specify how data from a data source should be displayed in a control. For example, you can bind a TextBox control's Text property to a specific field in a data source.

- **Two-Way Binding:** WinForms supports two-way data binding, which means changes made by the user in a bound control are reflected back to the underlying data source, and vice versa.

- **Formatting and Validation:** You can apply formatting and validation rules to data binding to ensure that data is presented correctly and meets specified criteria.

User Interface Customization

WinForms provides a wide range of controls and components for building the user interface of your application. You can customize these controls in various ways to create a visually appealing and user-friendly experience. Some common techniques include:

- **Control Styling:** You can change the appearance of controls using properties like BackColor, ForeColor, and Font. You can also apply custom styles through CSS in web-based WinForms applications.

- **Layout and Docking:** WinForms supports layout management using containers like Panel, TableLayoutPanel, and FlowLayoutPanel. You can control the arrangement of controls within these containers.

- **Localization:** To make your application accessible to a global audience, you can implement localization and resource files to provide translations for different languages.

- **Accessibility:** Ensure that your application is accessible to users with disabilities by setting control properties, providing meaningful descriptions, and supporting keyboard navigation.

In the next section, we will explore the integration of Windows Presentation Foundation (WPF) in VB.NET, which offers even more advanced capabilities for creating modern desktop applications with rich user interfaces.

Section 11.3: Integrating WPF in VB.NET

In this section, we will explore the integration of Windows Presentation Foundation (WPF) into your Visual Basic .NET (VB.NET) desktop applications. WPF is a powerful framework for building modern and visually appealing user interfaces, and it provides a more flexible and sophisticated approach compared to traditional Windows Forms (WinForms).

Understanding WPF

WPF is a part of the .NET Framework and is designed to provide a unified framework for building Windows applications that can run on both Windows desktop and web platforms. It introduces a new way of creating user interfaces using a markup language called XAML (eXtensible Application Markup Language) combined with a rich set of controls and styles.

Key advantages of WPF include:

1. **XAML:** With XAML, you can define your application's user interface declaratively, separating the UI from the application logic. This enables designers and developers to work on the UI independently.

2. **Rich Controls:** WPF provides a wide range of controls, including data-bound controls, 2D and 3D graphics, and multimedia elements. These controls are highly customizable and support rich styling and templating.

3. **Data Binding:** WPF has a powerful data binding system that simplifies connecting your user interface to data sources. You can bind UI elements directly to data objects and have the UI automatically update when the data changes.

4. **Styles and Templates:** WPF allows you to define styles and templates for controls, making it easy to create consistent and visually appealing UIs. Styles define the look and feel of controls, while templates define their structure.

5. **Resolution Independence:** WPF applications are resolution-independent, meaning they can adapt to different screen sizes and resolutions. This is essential for building applications that run on various devices.

6. **Graphics and Multimedia:** WPF includes a powerful graphics and media framework that allows you to create stunning visual effects, animations, and multimedia presentations.

Integrating WPF with VB.NET

Integrating WPF into a VB.NET application involves the following steps:

1. **Add References:** To use WPF in your VB.NET project, you need to add references to the necessary assemblies. The primary assembly for WPF is `PresentationCore.dll`.

2. **Create a WPF Window:** In your VB.NET code, you can create and display WPF windows just like you would with WinForms windows. WPF windows typically have a `.xaml` file for defining the UI layout.

3. **XAML Markup:** Define the user interface of your WPF window using XAML markup. You can use the Visual Studio designer to design the UI visually or edit the XAML directly.

4. **Code-Behind:** You can write VB.NET code-behind for your WPF window to handle events, interact with data, and perform application logic. The code-behind is associated with the XAML file.

5. **Data Binding:** Take advantage of WPF's powerful data binding capabilities to connect your UI elements to data sources, such as databases or collections.

Here's a simple example of a WPF window integrated into a VB.NET application:

```
<Window x:Class="WpfIntegration.MainWindow"
        xmlns="http://schemas.microsoft.com/winfx/2006/xaml/presentation"
        xmlns:x="http://schemas.microsoft.com/winfx/2006/xaml"
        Title="WPF Integration" Height="350" Width="525">
    <Grid>
        <TextBlock HorizontalAlignment="Center" VerticalAlignment="Center" Fo
ntSize="24">
            Welcome to WPF Integration!
        </TextBlock>
    </Grid>
</Window>
```

In the code-behind (`MainWindow.xaml.vb`), you can handle events or perform additional logic:

```
Class MainWindow
    Public Sub New()
        InitializeComponent()
    End Sub
End Class
```

This simple example shows the basics of integrating WPF into a VB.NET application. WPF's capabilities extend far beyond this, allowing you to create rich and interactive user interfaces for your desktop applications.

Section 11.4: Building Windows Services

In this section, we will explore the concept of Windows Services in the context of Visual Basic .NET (VB.NET) desktop application development. Windows Services, often referred to as system services or background services, are long-running processes that run in the background on Windows operating systems without the need for user interaction. They are essential for tasks like server applications, daemons, and scheduled tasks.

Windows Services are a fundamental part of the Windows operating system, and they can perform various tasks, such as:

1. **Background Processing:** Windows Services can execute tasks in the background without the need for a user to be logged in. This makes them suitable for tasks like data synchronization, file processing, and system monitoring.

2. **Server Applications:** Services can be used to implement server applications that listen for incoming network requests and provide services to clients. For example, a web server or a database server can be implemented as a Windows Service.

3. **Scheduled Tasks:** Services can run on a predefined schedule, making them suitable for automating repetitive tasks, such as backups, report generation, and maintenance.

4. **Custom Daemons:** You can create custom daemons that perform specialized tasks unique to your application or system.

Creating a Windows Service in VB.NET involves the following steps:

1. **Create a Windows Service Project:** Start by creating a new Windows Service project in Visual Studio. Visual Studio provides a template for creating Windows Services.

2. **Design the Service:** Define the functionality of your service by writing VB.NET code. A Windows Service typically overrides methods such as OnStart, OnStop, and OnPause to control its behavior.

3. **Installer Component:** To install and manage your service, you should add an installer component to your project. This component provides an easy way to install, start, stop, and uninstall the service.

4. **Configure Service Properties:** You can configure various properties of your service, such as its display name, description, and startup type (automatic, manual, or disabled).

5. **Build and Install:** Build your service project and install it using the InstallUtil utility provided by the .NET Framework. This utility registers your service with the Windows Service Control Manager (SCM).

Here's a simplified example of a Windows Service in VB.NET:

```vbnet
Imports System.ServiceProcess

Public Class MyService
    Inherits ServiceBase

    Protected Overrides Sub OnStart(ByVal args() As String)
        ' Add code here to start your service.
    End Sub

    Protected Overrides Sub OnStop()
        ' Add code here to stop your service.
    End Sub

    Public Sub New()
        Me.ServiceName = "MyService"
    End Sub

    Public Shared Sub Main()
        ServiceBase.Run(New MyService())
    End Sub
End Class
```

In this example, the MyService class inherits from ServiceBase, and its OnStart and OnStop methods can be customized to perform specific actions when the service starts and stops.

Deploying and Managing Windows Services

Once you have created a Windows Service, you can deploy it to a target machine. To manage Windows Services, you can use the Services MMC (Microsoft Management Console) or command-line utilities like sc.exe to start, stop, and configure services.

Windows Services are a powerful way to run background tasks and server applications on Windows machines. They provide reliability and can be set to run automatically when the system starts, making them suitable for various scenarios in desktop application development.

Section 11.5: Deployment and Distribution Strategies

In this section, we will explore deployment and distribution strategies for Visual Basic .NET (VB.NET) desktop applications. Deploying an application involves preparing it for distribution and making it available to users. Proper deployment ensures that your application runs smoothly on end-users' machines and can be updated or uninstalled as needed.

There are several methods for deploying VB.NET desktop applications, depending on your target audience and requirements:

1. **ClickOnce Deployment:** ClickOnce is a deployment technology that simplifies the installation and updating of VB.NET applications. It allows you to publish your application to a web server or network share and provides automatic update functionality. ClickOnce is suitable for applications distributed within an organization or to a limited number of users.

2. **MSI Installer:** Windows Installer (MSI) is a robust deployment method that provides full control over the installation process. You can create MSI installers using tools like WiX (Windows Installer XML) or commercial products like InstallShield. MSI installers are suitable for complex applications that require precise installation and configuration.

3. **XCopy Deployment:** For simple applications, you can use XCopy deployment, which involves copying application files to the target machine. XCopy deployment is straightforward but lacks features like automatic updates and advanced configuration.

4. **Windows Store (UWP) Deployment:** If you are developing Universal Windows Platform (UWP) apps, you can publish them to the Microsoft Store. This allows users to discover and install your app directly from the store.

5. **.NET Core and .NET 5+ Self-Contained Deployment:** If you are developing with .NET Core or .NET 5+, you can create self-contained deployments. This includes the .NET runtime with your application, making it independent of the system's installed .NET runtime version.

Application Signing and Security

When deploying VB.NET applications, it's important to consider security. Code signing ensures that your application hasn't been tampered with and can help establish trust with users and IT administrators. You can obtain a code signing certificate from a trusted certificate authority (CA) and use it to sign your application's executable files.

Additionally, consider security best practices, such as applying the principle of least privilege to your application and implementing proper data encryption and access control mechanisms.

Updating and Maintenance

Regular updates and maintenance are essential for keeping your VB.NET desktop application secure and bug-free. If you're using ClickOnce deployment, it provides automatic update capabilities. For other deployment methods, you may need to implement an update mechanism manually.

Maintaining clear versioning and release notes can help users understand the changes in each update. Additionally, consider providing user-friendly error messages and feedback mechanisms for users to report issues.

User Documentation and Support

Accompanying your VB.NET desktop application with user documentation is crucial for a positive user experience. Provide clear and concise instructions on how to install, configure, and use your application. Consider offering online help, FAQs, and support channels for users to seek assistance if needed.

Licensing and Activation

If your application requires licensing or activation, implement a secure and user-friendly mechanism. Ensure that the licensing process is transparent, and users can easily activate their copies of the application. Handle license management and validation in a way that minimizes the risk of piracy.

Distribution Channels

Finally, determine the distribution channels for your application. Will it be distributed through your website, a software marketplace, or an internal network? Each channel may have specific requirements and considerations, so choose the one that aligns with your target audience and goals.

In conclusion, successful deployment and distribution of your VB.NET desktop application involve careful planning, security considerations, user documentation, and a reliable update mechanism. By following best practices, you can ensure a smooth user experience and maintain the integrity of your application throughout its lifecycle.

Chapter 12: VB.NET and Cloud Computing

Section 12.1: Cloud Concepts and Services

In this section, we'll delve into the world of cloud computing and how Visual Basic .NET (VB.NET) developers can leverage cloud services to build scalable and flexible applications. Cloud computing has transformed the way applications are developed, deployed, and managed, offering a wide range of services that cater to various needs.

Understanding Cloud Computing

Cloud computing is a technology paradigm that involves delivering computing services (such as servers, storage, databases, networking, software, analytics, and intelligence) over the internet to offer faster innovation, flexible resources, and economies of scale. It eliminates the need for organizations to own and maintain physical hardware and software infrastructure, allowing them to focus on their core business.

Key concepts in cloud computing include:

- **On-Demand Self-Service:** Users can provision and manage resources as needed without requiring human intervention from the service provider.

- **Broad Network Access:** Cloud services are accessible over the internet via various devices, such as laptops, smartphones, and tablets.

- **Resource Pooling:** Cloud providers use multi-tenant models to serve multiple customers while ensuring data segregation, scalability, and resource optimization.

- **Rapid Elasticity:** Cloud resources can be quickly scaled up or down to accommodate varying workloads and demand.

- **Measured Service:** Users pay for cloud resources based on their usage, promoting cost efficiency.

Cloud Service Models

Cloud computing offers several service models, including:

1. **Infrastructure as a Service (IaaS):** IaaS provides virtualized computing resources over the internet. Users can rent virtual machines, storage, and networking components. VB.NET developers can deploy applications on IaaS platforms and have full control over the operating system and software stack.

2. **Platform as a Service (PaaS):** PaaS abstracts the infrastructure layer, allowing developers to focus solely on building and deploying applications. Cloud providers manage the underlying infrastructure, including operating systems, databases, and middleware. VB.NET developers can deploy web applications and services on PaaS platforms without worrying about infrastructure management.

3. **Software as a Service (SaaS):** SaaS delivers fully functional software applications over the internet. Users access software through a web browser without needing to install or maintain it locally. VB.NET developers can build SaaS applications to offer software services to users worldwide.

Cloud Deployment Models

Cloud computing also offers different deployment models:

1. **Public Cloud:** Public cloud services are owned and operated by third-party cloud service providers and are made available to the general public. Users can access resources and services on a pay-as-you-go basis. Popular public cloud providers include Amazon Web Services (AWS), Microsoft Azure, and Google Cloud Platform (GCP).

2. **Private Cloud:** Private cloud services are dedicated to a single organization and are not shared with other customers. Private clouds offer greater control, security, and customization options but require significant infrastructure investment.

3. **Hybrid Cloud:** Hybrid cloud combines public and private cloud resources, allowing data and applications to be shared between them. This model offers flexibility and scalability while maintaining control over sensitive data.

Benefits of Cloud Computing for VB.NET Developers

VB.NET developers can leverage cloud computing to:

- **Scalability:** Easily scale applications up or down based on demand, ensuring optimal performance.

- **Cost Efficiency:** Pay only for the resources and services you use, reducing upfront infrastructure costs.

- **Global Reach:** Deploy applications globally, reaching a broader audience.

- **Managed Services:** Use managed services and databases to offload routine maintenance tasks.

- **Security and Compliance:** Leverage cloud provider security features and certifications to enhance application security and compliance.

In the following sections, we will explore how VB.NET developers can work with various cloud services, including cloud storage, databases, and deployment strategies, to harness the power of cloud computing.

Section 12.2: Building Cloud-Enabled Applications

In this section, we will dive into the practical aspects of building cloud-enabled applications using Visual Basic .NET (VB.NET) and various cloud services. Cloud-enabled applications are designed to leverage the power and scalability of cloud computing while providing flexibility and reliability to users.

Choosing the Right Cloud Provider

Before you begin building cloud-enabled applications, it's essential to choose the right cloud provider that aligns with your project's requirements. Some of the leading cloud providers include Amazon Web Services (AWS), Microsoft Azure, Google Cloud Platform (GCP), and others. Each cloud provider offers a wide range of services and tools for different use cases.

Consider factors such as:

- **Service Offerings:** Assess the services offered by each cloud provider, such as computing, storage, databases, AI/ML, and more.

- **Pricing:** Understand the pricing model, including pay-as-you-go, reserved instances, and free tiers, to manage costs effectively.

- **Global Reach:** Evaluate the availability of data centers in regions that match your application's target audience.

- **Integration:** Ensure the cloud provider's services can seamlessly integrate with your VB.NET application.

Cloud-Ready Application Architecture

To build a cloud-enabled VB.NET application, you should adopt cloud-ready architecture principles. This architecture should emphasize scalability, fault tolerance, security, and efficiency. Some key architectural patterns to consider include:

- **Microservices:** Decompose your application into smaller, independently deployable services that can be scaled individually.

- **Serverless:** Consider using serverless computing platforms, such as AWS Lambda or Azure Functions, for event-driven, highly scalable workloads.

- **Containers:** Use containerization technologies like Docker and Kubernetes for consistent deployment across different cloud environments.

- **Auto-Scaling:** Implement auto-scaling policies to handle varying workloads gracefully.

Cloud Storage

One of the fundamental services offered by cloud providers is cloud storage. You can use cloud storage for various purposes, such as storing application data, user files, backups, and more. Cloud storage services typically provide scalability, durability, and accessibility. For instance:

- **Amazon S3:** AWS offers Amazon Simple Storage Service (S3), a highly scalable object storage service. You can use it to store and retrieve data, host static websites, and enable data archival.

- **Azure Blob Storage:** Microsoft Azure provides Azure Blob Storage, which is optimized for storing unstructured data. You can use it for multimedia files, backups, and data archiving.

- **Google Cloud Storage:** GCP offers Google Cloud Storage, a scalable and secure object storage service suitable for various data types, including binary data and multimedia.

VB.NET developers can integrate these cloud storage services into their applications using SDKs and libraries provided by the respective cloud providers. This enables you to offload data management and storage infrastructure concerns to the cloud.

Database Services

Cloud providers offer managed database services, which simplify database administration tasks, such as provisioning, patching, and backups. VB.NET developers can choose from various database options, including:

- **Relational Databases:** Cloud providers offer managed relational databases like Amazon RDS, Azure SQL Database, and Google Cloud SQL, which support popular database engines like SQL Server, MySQL, and PostgreSQL.

- **NoSQL Databases:** For applications requiring flexibility and scalability, cloud providers offer NoSQL databases like Amazon DynamoDB, Azure Cosmos DB, and Google Cloud Firestore.

- **Serverless Databases:** Consider serverless database options for on-demand scaling and cost efficiency. AWS Aurora Serverless and Azure SQL Database Serverless are examples.

Cloud Deployment and Scalability

Deploying VB.NET applications to the cloud involves configuring virtual machines, containers, or serverless functions based on your chosen cloud architecture. You can use infrastructure-as-code (IaC) tools like AWS CloudFormation, Azure Resource Manager (ARM) templates, or Terraform to define your application's infrastructure.

When deploying to the cloud, consider implementing load balancing, auto-scaling, and monitoring solutions to ensure your application can handle increasing traffic and workloads. Cloud providers offer services like AWS Elastic Load Balancing (ELB), Azure Load Balancer, and Google Cloud Load Balancing for this purpose.

Security is paramount when building cloud-enabled applications. Cloud providers offer a range of security tools and services to help protect your applications and data. Key security considerations include:

- **Identity and Access Management (IAM):** Use IAM services to control access to cloud resources. Ensure that the principle of least privilege is followed for users and services.

- **Encryption:** Encrypt data at rest and in transit using the encryption services provided by the cloud provider. This includes using SSL/TLS for data in transit and services like AWS Key Management Service (KMS) or Azure Key Vault for data at rest.

- **Network Security:** Implement network security groups, firewalls, and security rules to restrict inbound and outbound traffic to your cloud resources.

- **Compliance:** Ensure that your application complies with industry-specific regulations and standards. Cloud providers often provide compliance certifications to simplify this process.

In the upcoming sections of this chapter, we will explore practical examples and code snippets to demonstrate how VB.NET developers can implement cloud-ready architectures, work with cloud storage

Section 12.3: Cloud Storage and Data Services

In this section, we will delve into cloud storage and data services, focusing on how Visual Basic .NET (VB.NET) developers can leverage these services to store and manage data in cloud environments. Cloud storage and data services are essential components of modern cloud-based applications, providing scalability, durability, and accessibility to your data.

Cloud Storage Services

Cloud providers offer various cloud storage services that allow you to store and manage data, ranging from structured databases to unstructured files and objects. Here are some key aspects of cloud storage services:

- **Amazon S3 (Simple Storage Service):** Amazon Web Services (AWS) provides Amazon S3, an object storage service designed for scalability and data durability. You can use it to store and retrieve data objects, host static websites, and enable data archival.

- **Azure Blob Storage:** Microsoft Azure offers Azure Blob Storage, a scalable and secure object storage service. It's optimized for storing unstructured data like images, documents, videos, and backups.

- **Google Cloud Storage:** Google Cloud Platform (GCP) includes Google Cloud Storage, which provides a scalable and cost-effective way to store and manage various types of data, including binary data and multimedia files.

VB.NET developers can access these cloud storage services using SDKs (Software Development Kits) and APIs provided by the respective cloud providers. These SDKs simplify interactions with cloud storage, allowing you to upload, download, and manage objects or files programmatically.

Data Management and Databases

In addition to cloud storage, cloud providers offer managed database services, which significantly simplify database administration tasks. These services include:

- **Relational Databases:** Cloud providers offer managed relational database services, supporting popular database engines like SQL Server, MySQL, PostgreSQL, and Oracle. Examples include Amazon RDS, Azure SQL Database, and Google Cloud SQL.

- **NoSQL Databases:** For applications requiring flexibility and scalability, cloud providers provide NoSQL databases like Amazon DynamoDB, Azure Cosmos DB, and Google Cloud Firestore. These databases are suitable for unstructured or semi-structured data.

- **Serverless Databases:** Consider serverless database options for cost efficiency and on-demand scaling. Examples include AWS Aurora Serverless and Azure SQL Database Serverless.

VB.NET developers can connect to these managed databases using ADO.NET or other database drivers. You'll need to provide connection strings, credentials, and other configuration details to establish connections and interact with these databases.

Cloud Data Warehouses

Cloud data warehouses are specialized services for analytical data processing and reporting. They are designed to handle large volumes of data and complex queries efficiently. Key cloud data warehousing services include:

- **Amazon Redshift:** AWS offers Amazon Redshift, a fully managed data warehouse that allows you to run complex queries and perform analytics on large datasets.

- **Azure Synapse Analytics (formerly SQL Data Warehouse):** Microsoft Azure provides Azure Synapse Analytics, a data warehousing service that combines big data and data warehousing capabilities for analytics.

- **Google BigQuery:** GCP offers Google BigQuery, a serverless, highly scalable, and cost-effective multi-cloud data warehouse for running fast, SQL-like queries on large datasets.

VB.NET developers can use SQL clients and libraries to connect to these data warehouses and execute analytical queries. It's essential to design data warehouse schemas and queries that optimize performance for your specific analytical tasks.

Data Transfer and ETL (Extract, Transform, Load)

Moving data to and from the cloud is a common requirement in cloud-based applications. Cloud providers offer various tools and services to facilitate data transfer and ETL processes:

- **AWS DataSync:** AWS DataSync is a data transfer service that simplifies moving data between on-premises storage and Amazon S3, Amazon EFS, or Amazon FSx for Windows File Server.

- **Azure Data Factory:** Microsoft Azure provides Azure Data Factory, a cloud-based data integration service for creating, scheduling, and orchestrating data pipelines.

- **Google Cloud Dataflow:** GCP offers Google Cloud Dataflow, a fully managed stream and batch data processing service that can be used for ETL tasks.

VB.NET developers can use SDKs and APIs to interact with these data transfer and ETL services, enabling seamless data integration between on-premises systems and cloud environments.

Data Security and Encryption

Data security is a critical concern when working with cloud storage and data services. Cloud providers offer robust security features, including:

- **Encryption:** Encrypt data at rest and in transit using encryption services provided by the cloud provider. This includes using SSL/TLS for data in transit and services like AWS Key Management Service (KMS), Azure Key Vault, or Google Cloud Key Management Service (KMS) for data at rest.

- **Identity and Access Management (IAM):** Use IAM services to control access to cloud resources. Ensure that the principle of least privilege is followed for users and services.

- **Compliance:** Ensure that your data storage and management practices comply with industry-specific regulations and standards. Cloud providers often provide compliance certifications to simplify this process.

VB.NET developers should follow best practices for securing data and access control. This includes managing API keys, implementing encryption, and adhering to authentication and authorization mechanisms provided by the cloud services they use.

In the subsequent chapters, we will explore practical examples and code snippets to demonstrate how VB.NET developers can effectively leverage these cloud storage and data services in

Section 12.4: Cloud Deployment and Scalability

In this section, we will focus on cloud deployment and scalability strategies for Visual Basic .NET (VB.NET) applications. Deploying applications to the cloud and ensuring they can scale effectively are critical aspects of modern cloud-based development.

Deployment to the Cloud

Deploying a VB.NET application to the cloud involves configuring and provisioning the necessary cloud resources to host the application. This process can vary depending on the cloud provider you choose (e.g., AWS, Azure, Google Cloud) and the type of application you're deploying. Here are some key considerations:

1. **Infrastructure as Code (IaC):** Embrace IaC principles using tools like AWS CloudFormation, Azure Resource Manager (ARM) templates, or Google Cloud Deployment Manager. These tools allow you to define and provision cloud resources programmatically, ensuring consistency and repeatability.

2. **Virtual Machines (VMs):** For legacy applications or applications with specific configuration needs, you can deploy VB.NET applications on virtual machines (VMs) provided by cloud providers. You'll need to manage the VMs' operating systems and software.

3. **Containers:** Containerization with Docker and orchestration with Kubernetes offer portability and scalability advantages. You can package your VB.NET application into containers and deploy them using container orchestration platforms like Amazon ECS, Azure Kubernetes Service (AKS), or Google Kubernetes Engine (GKE).

4. **Serverless:** Consider serverless computing platforms like AWS Lambda, Azure Functions, or Google Cloud Functions for event-driven and scalable workloads. Serverless allows you to focus on code without managing infrastructure.

Scalability Strategies

Ensuring that your VB.NET application can scale to handle increasing workloads is essential for delivering a responsive user experience and optimizing costs. Here are strategies for achieving scalability:

1. **Load Balancing:** Implement load balancing to distribute incoming traffic across multiple instances of your application. Cloud providers offer load balancing services like AWS Elastic Load Balancing (ELB), Azure Load Balancer, and Google Cloud Load Balancing.

2. **Auto-Scaling:** Configure auto-scaling policies to automatically adjust the number of application instances based on metrics like CPU utilization, memory usage, or request rates. This ensures that your application can handle varying workloads.

3. **Caching:** Use caching solutions like Amazon ElastiCache, Azure Cache for Redis, or Google Cloud Memorystore to reduce the load on your application's backend by serving frequently accessed data from memory.

4. **Content Delivery Networks (CDNs):** Leverage CDNs such as AWS CloudFront, Azure Content Delivery Network (CDN), or Google Cloud CDN to distribute content globally and reduce latency for end-users.

5. **Database Scalability:** When using managed databases, configure them for horizontal scalability if supported. Consider using database sharding or partitioning to distribute data across multiple database instances.

6. **Serverless Components:** For serverless applications, design your functions or microservices to be stateless and independent, allowing them to scale automatically with demand.

Monitoring and Optimization

Scalability also involves continuous monitoring and optimization to ensure efficient resource utilization. Cloud providers offer monitoring and observability tools, and you can integrate them into your VB.NET applications:

1. **CloudWatch (AWS):** Use Amazon CloudWatch to collect and track metrics, collect and monitor log files, and set alarms. You can create custom metrics to monitor specific application performance indicators.

2. **Azure Monitor (Azure):** Azure Monitor provides a comprehensive solution for collecting, analyzing, and acting on telemetry data. It includes Application Insights for application performance monitoring.

3. **Stackdriver (Google Cloud):** Stackdriver Monitoring and Trace in Google Cloud offer performance and diagnostics data for applications running on Google Cloud.

Regularly review monitoring data to identify performance bottlenecks, adjust auto-scaling policies, and optimize resource allocation. Implement automated alerts to detect and respond to issues promptly.

Cost Management

Scalability should go hand-in-hand with cost management. Cloud resources are billed based on usage, so inefficiently scaled applications can lead to increased costs. Consider the following cost management strategies:

1. **Reserved Instances (RIs) or Savings Plans:** For predictable workloads, reserve cloud resources with RIs (AWS) or Savings Plans (Azure) to reduce costs compared to on-demand pricing.

2. **Spot Instances (AWS) or Low-Priority VMs (Azure):** Use spot instances or low-priority VMs for workloads that can tolerate interruptions. These instances are available at lower costs but can be preempted.

3. **Cost Explorer (AWS), Cost Management and Billing (Azure), and Cost Management (Google Cloud):** Utilize cloud providers' cost management tools to track and optimize spending.

4. **Resource Tagging:** Implement resource tagging to attribute costs to specific projects, teams, or purposes, making it easier to identify areas for cost optimization.

In summary, deploying VB.NET applications to the cloud and designing for scalability require careful planning and consideration of various cloud deployment options and scalability strategies. Continuously monitoring, optimizing, and managing costs are essential for efficient and cost-effective cloud operations.

Section 12.5: Challenges and Best Practices

In the final section of Chapter 12, we'll discuss some of the challenges and best practices associated with cloud computing in Visual Basic .NET (VB.NET) development. While cloud computing offers numerous benefits, it also comes with its own set of challenges that developers should be aware of.

Challenges

1. **Security Concerns:** Security is a top concern when moving applications and data to the cloud. Developers must implement strong security measures, such as encryption, access controls, and authentication, to protect data from unauthorized access.

2. **Data Privacy and Compliance:** Depending on the industry and location, there may be strict regulations governing data privacy and compliance. Developers need to ensure that their VB.NET applications comply with these regulations, which can vary significantly.

3. **Vendor Lock-In:** Cloud providers offer a range of services and tools that can be tightly integrated with applications. However, this can lead to vendor lock-in, making it challenging to migrate applications to another cloud provider in the future.

4. **Cost Management:** Without proper cost monitoring and optimization, cloud costs can spiral out of control. Developers must have mechanisms in place to track and control spending effectively.

5. **Distributed Systems Complexity:** Developing distributed systems, which are common in cloud applications, introduces complexity. Handling issues like data consistency, communication between services, and fault tolerance becomes crucial.

Best Practices

1. **Security-First Approach:** Prioritize security from the beginning of your VB.NET cloud project. Implement identity and access management (IAM) controls, encryption, and regular security audits.

2. **Data Backup and Recovery:** Implement robust data backup and recovery mechanisms to ensure data integrity and availability, even in the event of unexpected failures.

3. **Multi-Cloud Strategy:** Consider a multi-cloud strategy that involves using multiple cloud providers or hybrid cloud solutions. This reduces vendor lock-in and enhances resilience.

4. **Continuous Cost Optimization:** Continuously monitor cloud resource usage and costs. Leverage cost management tools provided by cloud providers and regularly review your architecture for optimization opportunities.

5. **DevOps Practices:** Adopt DevOps practices for automated deployment, testing, and continuous integration and delivery (CI/CD). This streamlines development and deployment processes.

6. **Microservices Architecture:** Consider breaking down your application into microservices. This architecture improves scalability and allows for more granular updates and maintenance.

7. **Serverless Computing:** Utilize serverless computing for event-driven workloads or functions that require automatic scaling. This can reduce operational overhead.

8. **Monitoring and Observability:** Implement comprehensive monitoring and observability solutions to gain insights into the performance and health of your VB.NET applications. Use tools like application performance monitoring (APM) and distributed tracing.

9. **Documentation and Training:** Document your cloud architecture and best practices, and ensure your development team receives proper training on cloud technologies and security protocols.

10. **Compliance Management:** Stay informed about data privacy and compliance regulations that affect your application. Implement features and controls to adhere to these regulations.

11. **Disaster Recovery Planning:** Develop a disaster recovery plan that includes backup strategies, redundancy, and failover mechanisms to ensure business continuity.

12. **Regular Testing:** Perform regular load testing and stress testing to validate the scalability and resilience of your cloud-deployed VB.NET applications.

By adhering to these best practices and addressing the associated challenges, you can develop robust and secure VB.NET applications in the cloud. Cloud computing continues to evolve, offering new opportunities and challenges, so staying informed and adaptable is essential for successful cloud development.

Chapter 13: Interoperability with Other Languages

Interoperability is a critical aspect of modern software development, allowing different programming languages and technologies to work together seamlessly. In this chapter, we will explore how Visual Basic .NET (VB.NET) can interoperate with other languages, enabling you to leverage existing code, libraries, and components written in languages such as C/C++, Java, and more. Interoperability opens up new possibilities for extending your VB.NET applications and integrating with a broader ecosystem of software.

Section 13.1: Working with COM Components

Component Object Model (COM) is a binary-interface standard for software components introduced by Microsoft. It enables software written in different languages to communicate and interact with each other. VB.NET provides robust support for working with COM components, making it possible to use legacy COM libraries and services in your .NET applications.

To work with COM components in VB.NET, you can follow these steps:

1. **Register the COM Component:** First, ensure that the COM component is registered on your system. Registration provides information about the component's location and interfaces to the system.

2. **Add a Reference:** In your VB.NET project, add a reference to the COM component. You can do this by right-clicking on References in the Solution Explorer, selecting "Add Reference," and then browsing for the COM component's registered DLL or executable.

3. **Import the Namespace:** In your VB.NET code, import the namespace associated with the COM component to access its types and members.

4. **Create and Use COM Objects:** You can now create instances of COM objects and call their methods or access properties, just like any other .NET objects.

Here's a simple example of working with a COM component in VB.NET:

```
Imports MyCOMNamespace ' Replace with the actual COM component's namespace

Module MainModule
    Sub Main()
        Dim comObject As New MyCOMClass() ' Replace with the actual COM class
name
        comObject.SomeMethod() ' Call a method of the COM component
        Dim result As Integer = comObject.SomeProperty ' Access a property of
the COM component
        Console.WriteLine($"Result: {result}")
```

```
    End Sub
End Module
```

Keep in mind that COM interop in VB.NET allows you to use COM components, but it does not enable you to work with .NET Core or .NET 5+ applications, as these frameworks do not support COM components.

In the following sections, we'll explore more ways to interoperate with other languages and technologies, including integrating with C/C++ and Java, using P/Invoke for native calls, and conducting cross-language debugging and testing. These techniques will expand your VB.NET application's capabilities and compatibility with a wide range of systems and libraries.

Section 13.2: Integrating with C/C++ and .NET Languages

Integrating Visual Basic .NET (VB.NET) with other programming languages can be a powerful way to leverage existing code, libraries, and expertise. In this section, we'll focus on integrating VB.NET with C/C++ and other .NET languages like C# and F#. Each of these languages has its strengths, and interoperability enables you to choose the best tool for each part of your application.

Calling Native Code with P/Invoke

Platform Invocation Services (P/Invoke) is a mechanism provided by .NET that allows managed code (such as VB.NET) to call unmanaged code written in languages like C and C++. This is particularly useful when you want to use native libraries or system APIs in your VB.NET application.

To use P/Invoke in VB.NET, follow these steps:

1. **Declare the External Method:** Define a DllImport attribute to declare the external method you want to call. This attribute specifies the name of the DLL containing the unmanaged code and the method's signature.

2. **Import the Namespace:** Import the System.Runtime.InteropServices namespace, which contains the necessary classes and attributes for P/Invoke.

3. **Call the Native Method:** You can now call the native method just like any other .NET method.

Here's a simple example of using P/Invoke to call the Windows API's MessageBox function:

```
Imports System.Runtime.InteropServices

Public Module MainModule
    ' Declare the external method from user32.dll
    <DllImport("user32.dll", CharSet:=CharSet.Auto)>
    Public Function MessageBox(hWnd As IntPtr, text As String, caption As Str
```

```
ing, options As Integer) As Integer
    End Function

    Sub Main()
        ' Call the MessageBox function
        MessageBox(IntPtr.Zero, "Hello, P/Invoke!", "Message", 0)
    End Sub
End Module
```

Interoperability with Other .NET Languages

VB.NET is part of the .NET ecosystem, which includes languages like C# and F#. These languages are designed to work seamlessly together, sharing the same runtime and libraries. This means you can create libraries and components in one language and use them in another.

To use a library written in another .NET language in your VB.NET project:

1. **Add a Reference:** Add a reference to the compiled library (DLL) or project containing the code you want to use. This can be done through the Visual Studio project settings or by manually referencing the DLL.

2. **Import the Namespace:** Import the appropriate namespace or module from the library.

3. **Use the Types:** You can now use the types and methods from the referenced library as if they were part of your VB.NET project.

Here's an example of referencing a C# library in a VB.NET project:

```
Imports MyCSharpLibrary ' Replace with the actual C# library's namespace

Module MainModule
    Sub Main()
        Dim myObject As New MyClassFromCSharp()
        myObject.DoSomething() ' Call a method from the C# library
    End Sub
End Module
```

In summary, integrating VB.NET with C/C++ and other .NET languages is a valuable capability that allows you to leverage existing code and combine the strengths of different languages to build robust and feature-rich applications. Whether you're calling native code with P/Invoke or using libraries from other .NET languages, interoperability widens the possibilities for your VB.NET projects.

Section 13.3: Using P/Invoke for Native Calls

Platform Invocation Services (P/Invoke) is a powerful feature in .NET that allows managed code to call unmanaged code, typically written in languages like C or C++. This is especially useful when you need to interact with native libraries, system APIs, or other low-level functionality from within your Visual Basic .NET (VB.NET) application.

Here's a detailed look at how to use P/Invoke in VB.NET:

1. Declaration with DllImport Attribute

To use P/Invoke, you start by declaring the external method you want to call using the DllImport attribute. This attribute provides information about the native function, such as its name and the DLL (Dynamic Link Library) or shared library that contains it. You also specify the calling convention and other details.

Here's a simple example of declaring and using P/Invoke to call the Windows API's MessageBox function:

```
Imports System.Runtime.InteropServices

Public Class MainClass
    ' Declare the external method from user32.dll
    <DllImport("user32.dll", CharSet:=CharSet.Auto)>
    Public Shared Function MessageBox(hWnd As IntPtr, text As String, caption
As String, options As Integer) As Integer
    End Function

    Public Shared Sub Main()
        ' Call the MessageBox function
        MessageBox(IntPtr.Zero, "Hello, P/Invoke!", "Message", 0)
    End Sub
End Class
```

In this example, the DllImport attribute is used to declare the MessageBox function from the user32.dll library. The function can then be called like any other method within your VB.NET code.

2. Import Required Namespaces

To use P/Invoke effectively, you need to import the System.Runtime.InteropServices namespace, which contains the classes and attributes needed for P/Invoke. This allows you to access the DllImport attribute and other related types.

3. Specify the Function Signature

When declaring an external function using `DllImport`, you need to specify its signature, including the return type and parameters. Ensure that the signature matches the native function's signature exactly, including the parameter types, order, and names.

4. Call the Native Function

Once you've declared the external function, you can call it like any other method in your VB.NET code. Pass the required parameters, and the P/Invoke mechanism will handle the transition between managed and unmanaged code.

P/Invoke provides a bridge between the managed world of VB.NET and the unmanaged world of native code, allowing you to harness the power of existing libraries and system APIs within your VB.NET applications. It's a valuable tool for tasks like working with hardware, system services, or legacy code that isn't available in managed form.

Section 13.4: VB.NET and Java Integration

Integrating Visual Basic .NET (VB.NET) with Java can be a valuable approach when you need to leverage existing Java libraries or work with Java components in your VB.NET applications. This section explores various methods and tools to achieve seamless interoperability between VB.NET and Java.

Java Interoperability Options

1. Java Native Interface (JNI)

The **Java Native Interface (JNI)** is a standard programming interface for Java that allows Java code running in a Java Virtual Machine (JVM) to call and be called by native applications, which may be written in C, C++, or other languages. To use JNI from VB.NET, you need to create a Java wrapper for the Java code you want to access, compile it into a Java library (a JAR file), and then use P/Invoke to call the JNI functions from VB.NET. While this approach provides low-level access, it can be complex and error-prone.

2. Java-to-.NET Bridges

Several third-party tools and libraries provide bridges between Java and .NET. One popular option is **IKVM.NET**, which is an open-source implementation of Java for Mono and the Microsoft .NET Framework. With IKVM.NET, you can run Java applications on the .NET platform and even mix Java and .NET code within the same application. This simplifies integration but may require adjustments to your existing Java code.

3. Web Services and REST APIs

When dealing with remote Java services, exposing Java functionality as web services or RESTful APIs is a common approach. VB.NET can then consume these services using standard HTTP requests. This approach abstracts the underlying Java implementation and allows for platform-independent communication.

Example: Consuming a Java Web Service

Here's a simplified example of how you can consume a Java web service from a VB.NET application:

```vbnet
Imports System.Net
Imports System.IO
Imports System.Text

Public Class MainClass
    Public Shared Sub Main()
        Dim url As String = "http://example.com/javaws/service"

        ' Create a web request
        Dim request As HttpWebRequest = WebRequest.Create(url)

        ' Set request properties (e.g., HTTP method, headers)
        request.Method = "GET"

        ' Send the request and get the response
        Using response As HttpWebResponse = DirectCast(request.GetResponse(),
HttpWebResponse)
            Using stream As Stream = response.GetResponseStream()
                Using reader As New StreamReader(stream, Encoding.UTF8)
                    Dim result As String = reader.ReadToEnd()
                    Console.WriteLine("Response from Java web service:")
                    Console.WriteLine(result)
                End Using
            End Using
        End Using
    End Sub
End Class
```

In this example, VB.NET makes an HTTP GET request to a Java web service's URL and receives a response that can be processed accordingly.

Considerations

When integrating VB.NET with Java, consider factors like data serialization, exception handling, and security. Ensure that the Java components you interact with are well-documented, and thoroughly test your integration to identify and address any issues that may arise.

While integrating VB.NET and Java can be complex, it provides a powerful way to combine the strengths of both platforms and reuse existing assets, ultimately enhancing the capabilities of your applications.

Section 13.5: Cross-Language Debugging and Testing

Debugging and testing are critical aspects of software development, and when working with multiple languages in the same project, it's essential to understand how to effectively debug and test code written in different languages. In this section, we'll explore strategies and tools for cross-language debugging and testing when integrating Visual Basic .NET (VB.NET) with other languages like Java, C/C++, and more.

Debugging Across Language Boundaries

Debugging across language boundaries can be challenging, as each programming language may have its debugging tools and techniques. Here are some general strategies to facilitate cross-language debugging:

1. Logging and Debug Output

One of the simplest ways to debug across languages is by using **logging** and **debug output**. You can instrument your code with log statements in both languages to capture information about the program's execution. Tools like log analyzers can help correlate log entries from different languages to identify issues.

2. Remote Debugging

Some integrated development environments (IDEs) and debugging tools support **remote debugging**. For example, you can set breakpoints in your VB.NET code and attach a debugger to a remote process running code in another language. This allows you to inspect variables, step through code, and identify issues across language boundaries.

3. Debugging Proxies

In some cases, you may need to create **debugging proxies** or **wrapper functions** in one language to facilitate debugging in another. These proxies can expose the inner workings of the code in a way that's more accessible to the debugging tools of the other language.

Testing Across Language Boundaries

Testing is another crucial aspect of software development, and it becomes more complex when dealing with multiple languages. Here's how you can approach testing across language boundaries:

1. Unit Testing

Unit testing is a valuable practice to ensure that individual components of your code work correctly. For code written in different languages, create unit tests in each language's testing framework. Ensure that your tests cover the expected behaviors of the components, taking into account the interactions between languages.

Integration testing focuses on verifying that different parts of your application work together as expected. When languages are integrated, perform integration tests that exercise the interaction points between them. Use test harnesses or scripts to orchestrate these tests.

3. Mocking and Stubs

In situations where it's challenging to test across languages, consider using **mocking** and **stubs**. Create mock objects or stubs for the components written in other languages to simulate their behavior during testing. This allows you to isolate the code you're testing.

Tools for Cross-Language Debugging and Testing

Several tools can assist with cross-language debugging and testing:

- **Visual Studio Debugger**: If you're working with VB.NET and other .NET languages like C#, the Visual Studio debugger supports debugging across languages.

- **GDB**: The GNU Debugger (GDB) is a powerful tool for debugging C/C++ code and can be used for debugging when working with mixed-language applications.

- **IDE Extensions**: Some integrated development environments offer extensions or plugins to facilitate cross-language debugging. For example, Visual Studio Code has extensions for debugging various languages.

- **Test Frameworks**: Use test frameworks that support multiple languages, such as JUnit for Java and NUnit for .NET, to create and execute tests across languages.

Conclusion

Cross-language debugging and testing are essential skills when working on projects that involve multiple programming languages. By employing the strategies and tools discussed in this section, you can effectively debug and test code written in different languages, ensuring the reliability and correctness of your applications.

Chapter 14: VB.NET for Mobile Development

Section 14.1: Introduction to Mobile App Development

Mobile app development has become a dominant force in the software industry due to the widespread use of smartphones and tablets. In this section, we'll introduce you to mobile app development with a focus on using Visual Basic .NET (VB.NET). We'll cover the fundamental concepts, platforms, and tools you need to get started in the world of mobile app development.

The Mobile App Ecosystem

Mobile app development encompasses a wide range of platforms, each with its ecosystem. Some of the most popular mobile platforms include:

- **iOS**: Apple's mobile operating system, primarily used on iPhones and iPads.
- **Android**: Google's mobile operating system, found on a vast array of smartphones and tablets.
- **Cross-Platform**: Frameworks like Xamarin and React Native allow you to write code that runs on multiple platforms with shared codebases.

Choosing a Development Approach

When embarking on mobile app development with VB.NET, you have several development approaches to consider:

1. Native App Development

Native app development involves creating apps for a specific platform, such as iOS or Android, using platform-specific languages and tools. While this approach provides the best performance and access to native device features, it requires separate development efforts for each platform.

2. Cross-Platform Development

Cross-platform development allows you to write code that can run on multiple platforms with a shared codebase. VB.NET developers can leverage frameworks like Xamarin, which allows you to write apps that work on iOS, Android, and other platforms using a single codebase.

3. Progressive Web Apps (PWAs)

Progressive Web Apps are web applications that provide an app-like experience through web browsers. While not native apps, PWAs are accessible across platforms and can be developed using web technologies like HTML, CSS, and JavaScript.

Tools for Mobile Development

To get started with mobile app development in VB.NET, you'll need the right tools:

- **Visual Studio**: Microsoft's Visual Studio is a powerful integrated development environment (IDE) that supports VB.NET and mobile app development. You can use it for native development and cross-platform development with Xamarin.

- **Xamarin**: Xamarin is a popular cross-platform development framework that allows you to write mobile apps in VB.NET and deploy them on iOS, Android, and other platforms. It provides a wide range of libraries and tools for building robust mobile applications.

Conclusion

Mobile app development is an exciting field that opens up opportunities to reach a vast user base through smartphones and tablets. In this section, we've introduced the mobile app ecosystem, development approaches, and the essential tools for getting started with mobile app development in VB.NET. Whether you choose native development or opt for cross-platform solutions like Xamarin, VB.NET can be a valuable language for building mobile applications.

Section 14.2: Xamarin and Cross-Platform Development

When it comes to developing mobile apps with VB.NET, Xamarin is a powerful framework that enables cross-platform development. In this section, we'll delve into Xamarin and how you can use it to create mobile applications that run on iOS, Android, and other platforms with a shared codebase.

What is Xamarin?

Xamarin is a cross-platform development framework that allows developers to write mobile apps using C# and .NET, including VB.NET. It provides a single codebase that can target multiple platforms, making it a valuable choice for efficient mobile app development.

Key Features of Xamarin:

1. Shared Codebase:

Xamarin allows you to write a significant portion of your app's code in C# or VB.NET, which can be shared across different platforms. This shared code includes business logic, data access, and more.

2. Native User Interfaces:

With Xamarin, you can create native user interfaces for each platform. This ensures that your app looks and feels like a native app, providing a seamless user experience.

3. Access to Native APIs:

Xamarin provides access to platform-specific APIs and libraries, allowing you to utilize device features like the camera, GPS, and sensors. You can also use third-party libraries and NuGet packages.

4. Visual Studio Integration:

Xamarin integrates seamlessly with Microsoft Visual Studio, making it easy for VB.NET developers to get started with mobile app development. Visual Studio provides a rich set of tools for designing, coding, debugging, and testing mobile apps.

5. Xamarin.Forms:

Xamarin.Forms is a UI toolkit that allows you to create shared user interfaces using XAML. It simplifies the process of building cross-platform apps by providing a common UI abstraction.

The Xamarin Development Workflow:

Developing mobile apps with Xamarin typically follows these steps:

1. **Project Setup**: Create a new Xamarin project in Visual Studio, choosing the appropriate project type for iOS, Android, or both.

2. **UI Design**: Design the user interface of your app, either using Xamarin.Forms for shared UI or platform-specific UI design.

3. **Coding**: Write the application logic in C# or VB.NET. Utilize shared code for common functionality and platform-specific code where necessary.

4. **Testing**: Use the built-in emulator or deploy the app to physical devices for testing. Xamarin provides excellent debugging tools.

5. **Deployment**: Once your app is ready, you can publish it to app stores like the Apple App Store and Google Play Store.

Benefits of Xamarin:

- **Code Reusability**: Xamarin allows you to maximize code reuse, saving time and effort in developing for multiple platforms.

- **Native Performance**: Xamarin apps offer native performance because they compile to native code. Users won't notice a significant difference between Xamarin and fully native apps.

- **Access to Device Features**: You can leverage device-specific features through Xamarin's bindings to native APIs.

- **Community and Resources**: Xamarin has a thriving developer community and extensive documentation, making it easier to find solutions to common challenges.

Conclusion:

Xamarin is a valuable tool for VB.NET developers looking to enter the world of mobile app development. With its ability to create cross-platform apps while maintaining a native look and feel, Xamarin simplifies the development process and offers excellent code reusability. Whether you're targeting iOS, Android, or both, Xamarin allows you to build high-quality mobile apps efficiently.

Section 14.3: Creating Mobile User Interfaces

In this section, we will explore the process of creating mobile user interfaces (UIs) for your VB.NET mobile apps using Xamarin. User interfaces play a crucial role in determining how users interact with your app, so designing a user-friendly and visually appealing UI is essential for the success of your mobile application.

Xamarin.Forms for Cross-Platform UIs

Xamarin.Forms is a UI toolkit that simplifies the creation of cross-platform user interfaces. It allows you to define your app's UI using a single XAML codebase, which can then be rendered differently on iOS, Android, and other platforms. Xamarin.Forms provides a wide range of UI controls and layouts that you can use to build your app's interface.

Here's a brief overview of key concepts related to creating mobile user interfaces with Xamarin.Forms:

XAML Markup:

XAML (eXtensible Application Markup Language) is a declarative markup language used to define the structure and appearance of your app's UI. It provides a clear separation between the UI and the code-behind logic, making it easier to work collaboratively and maintain your app.

Pages and Layouts:

In Xamarin.Forms, screens are represented as Pages. You can create different types of pages, such as ContentPage, MasterDetailPage, and TabbedPage, to structure your app's navigation and content presentation. Layouts like StackLayout, Grid, and AbsoluteLayout help you arrange UI elements.

Controls:

Xamarin.Forms offers a wide range of controls, including buttons, labels, text entry fields, images, and more. You can customize their appearance and behavior to match your app's design and functionality.

Data Binding:

Data binding in Xamarin.Forms allows you to connect UI elements to data sources, such as ViewModel classes, and automatically update the UI when the underlying data changes. This simplifies the process of displaying and managing data in your app.

Styles and Themes:

Xamarin.Forms supports styles and themes, making it easy to create a consistent and visually appealing UI design. You can define styles for UI elements and apply them throughout your app.

Platform-Specific Customization:

While Xamarin.Forms promotes code sharing, you can still implement platform-specific customizations when necessary. This allows you to take advantage of platform-specific features and design guidelines.

Designing Your Mobile UI

When designing your mobile UI, consider the following best practices:

- **User-Centered Design**: Understand your target audience and their needs. Design the UI with a focus on user experience (UX) to ensure that your app is intuitive and easy to use.

- **Responsive Design**: Create layouts that adapt to various screen sizes and orientations, ensuring a consistent experience on different devices.

- **Consistency**: Maintain a consistent design across your app to provide a cohesive look and feel. Use styles and templates to achieve this.

- **Performance**: Optimize your UI for performance by minimizing complex animations and unnecessary rendering. Use asynchronous loading for data-intensive UIs.

- **Testing**: Test your UI on different devices and platforms to identify and resolve any layout or usability issues.

Example XAML Code:

Here's a simple example of XAML code that defines a basic Xamarin.Forms page with a label and a button:

```
<ContentPage xmlns="http://xamarin.com/schemas/2014/forms"
             xmlns:x="http://schemas.microsoft.com/winfx/2009/xaml"
             x:Class="YourApp.MainPage">

    <StackLayout>
        <Label Text="Welcome to Xamarin.Forms!"
               VerticalOptions="CenterAndExpand"
```

```
                    HorizontalOptions="CenterAndExpand" />
        <Button Text="Click Me" Clicked="OnButtonClicked" />
    </StackLayout>
</ContentPage>
```

In this code, we have a `ContentPage` containing a `StackLayout` with a `Label` and a `Button`. The `x:Class` attribute links the XAML file to its code-behind file, allowing you to handle events and logic.

Conclusion:

Creating mobile user interfaces with Xamarin.Forms allows you to build cross-platform apps efficiently while delivering a native look and feel. With a good understanding of XAML markup, layouts, controls, data binding, and styling, you can design visually appealing and user-friendly interfaces for your VB.NET mobile applications.

Section 14.4: Accessing Device Features

In this section, we'll explore how to access device features and native functionalities in your VB.NET mobile applications developed with Xamarin. To provide a rich user experience, many mobile apps require interaction with device-specific features like the camera, location services, sensors, and more. Xamarin allows you to access these features through platform-specific APIs while maintaining code reusability.

Platform-Specific Code

Xamarin enables you to write platform-specific code when necessary to interact with device features. This is achieved through DependencyService, which provides a way to call platform-specific implementations from shared code. Here's a basic overview of how it works:

1. **Define an Interface**: In your shared code, define an interface that represents the functionality you want to access on each platform. For example, you can create an interface for accessing the device's camera.

2. **Implement on Each Platform**: In your platform-specific projects (iOS, Android, etc.), implement the interface with platform-specific code. This code will utilize the native APIs and features of each platform.

3. **DependencyService**: Use DependencyService to access the platform-specific implementation from your shared code. You can call methods and retrieve data through this interface.

Example: Accessing the Camera

Let's consider an example where you want to take a photo using the device's camera. First, define an interface in your shared code:

```
public interface ICameraService
{
    Task<byte[]> TakePhotoAsync();
}
```

Next, implement this interface on each platform. Here's a simplified example for Android using Xamarin.Android:

```
[assembly: Dependency(typeof(CameraService))]
namespace YourApp.Droid.Services
{
    public class CameraService : ICameraService
    {
        public async Task<byte[]> TakePhotoAsync()
        {
            // Implement camera access logic for Android
            // This may involve using Android's Camera2 API or third-party li
braries
            // Return the captured photo as a byte array
        }
    }
}
```

And here's a simplified example for iOS using Xamarin.iOS:

```
[assembly: Dependency(typeof(CameraService))]
namespace YourApp.iOS.Services
{
    public class CameraService : ICameraService
    {
        public async Task<byte[]> TakePhotoAsync()
        {
            // Implement camera access logic for iOS
            // This may involve using AVCaptureSession and related APIs
            // Return the captured photo as a byte array
        }
    }
}
```

In your shared code, you can now use DependencyService to take a photo:

```
var cameraService = DependencyService.Get<ICameraService>();
if (cameraService != null)
{
    byte[] photo = await cameraService.TakePhotoAsync();
    // Process and display the photo
}
```

Considerations

When working with platform-specific code, keep the following considerations in mind:

- **Permissions**: Accessing device features may require specific permissions. Ensure that you request and handle permissions appropriately.

- **Error Handling**: Implement error handling and graceful degradation in case a feature is not available on a specific platform.

- **Testing**: Test your app on different devices and platforms to ensure consistent behavior.

By following these principles and leveraging Xamarin's DependencyService, you can seamlessly integrate device-specific features into your VB.NET mobile applications, providing users with a more engaging and feature-rich experience.

Section 14.5: Deployment to Mobile Platforms

In this section, we will discuss the deployment of VB.NET mobile applications developed using Xamarin to various mobile platforms, including Android and iOS. Deploying your app to real devices or app stores is a critical step in making your application available to users. We'll cover the essential aspects of deployment, including app signing, distribution, and testing.

Android Deployment

1. APK Generation

For Android, Xamarin generates APK (Android Package) files, which are the installation packages for Android apps. To deploy your app to Android devices or the Google Play Store, you need to generate a signed APK. Here are the key steps:

- **Create a Keystore**: Generate a keystore file that securely stores your app's signing key.

- **Configure Xamarin Project**: In your Xamarin Android project settings, specify the keystore details, including the keystore file, alias, and password.

- **Build the Release APK**: Build the release version of your app, which is optimized and ready for deployment.

- **Sign the APK**: Sign the APK using your keystore. This ensures that users can verify the authenticity of your app.

2. Distribution

Once you have a signed APK, you can distribute your app through various channels:

- **Google Play Store**: Publish your app on the Google Play Store, where users can discover and install it.

- **Alternative App Stores**: You can also distribute your APK through alternative Android app stores.

- **Direct Distribution**: Share the APK directly with users via email, website downloads, or other distribution methods.

iOS Deployment

1. iOS App Store Deployment

For iOS, Xamarin generates an IPA (iOS App Store Package) file. To deploy your app to the Apple App Store, follow these steps:

- **Create an App ID**: Register your app with Apple Developer Program and create an App ID.

- **Generate Certificates**: Create distribution certificates and provisioning profiles for your app.

- **Configure Xamarin Project**: In your Xamarin iOS project settings, select the appropriate provisioning profile.

- **Build the IPA**: Build the release version of your app for iOS.

- **Submit to App Store**: Use Apple's App Store Connect to submit your app for review and distribution on the App Store.

2. Ad-Hoc Distribution

For testing purposes or limited distribution, you can create ad-hoc builds of your app. These builds can be installed on specific iOS devices without going through the App Store. Here are the steps:

- **Create Ad-Hoc Provisioning Profile**: Generate an ad-hoc provisioning profile for the specific devices.

- **Build the IPA**: Build your app with the ad-hoc provisioning profile.

- **Distribute the IPA**: Share the IPA file with the intended users, who can install it on their devices using Apple Configurator or Xcode.

Cross-Platform Considerations

While deploying VB.NET Xamarin apps to Android and iOS platforms, consider the following:

- **App Store Guidelines**: Ensure that your app complies with the guidelines and policies of the respective app stores.

- **Testing**: Thoroughly test your app on various Android and iOS devices to identify and resolve platform-specific issues.

- **Version Control**: Use version control systems like Git to manage your app's source code and track changes.

- **User Feedback**: Establish a system for gathering and responding to user feedback, including bug reports and feature requests.

By following these deployment practices, you can successfully distribute your VB.NET Xamarin mobile app to Android and iOS users, making it accessible to a wider audience.

Chapter 15: Security and Authentication in VB.NET

Section 15.1: Authentication and Authorization

Security is a critical aspect of software development, and it's essential to ensure that your VB.NET applications are secure. One of the fundamental components of application security is authentication and authorization. Authentication is the process of verifying the identity of a user, while authorization determines what actions a user is allowed to perform within the application.

Authentication

In VB.NET, authentication can be implemented using various techniques. The most common method is through username and password verification. Here's a simplified example of how you can perform username and password authentication:

```
Imports System.Security.Cryptography

Public Class AuthenticationManager
    Public Function AuthenticateUser(username As String, password As String)
As Boolean
        ' In a real application, you would fetch the user's hashed password f
rom a database.
        Dim hashedPasswordFromDatabase As String = GetHashedPasswordFromDatab
ase(username)

        ' Hash the provided password using the same algorithm and compare it
with the stored hash.
        Dim hashedPassword As String = HashPassword(password)

        ' Compare the two hashed passwords for authentication.
        Return String.Compare(hashedPassword, hashedPasswordFromDatabase) = 0
    End Function

    Private Function HashPassword(password As String) As String
        ' Use a secure hashing algorithm like SHA-256.
        Using sha256 As New SHA256Managed()
            Dim bytes As Byte() = Encoding.UTF8.GetBytes(password)
            Dim hashBytes As Byte() = sha256.ComputeHash(bytes)
            Return BitConverter.ToString(hashBytes).Replace("-", "").ToLower(
)
        End Using
    End Function

    ' Implement a method to retrieve the hashed password from the database.
    Private Function GetHashedPasswordFromDatabase(username As String) As Str
ing
```

```vbnet
        ' Retrieve the hashed password for the given username.
        ' In a real application, this would involve a database query.
        ' Return the hashed password stored in the database.
        Return "hashedPasswordFromDatabase"
    End Function
End Class
```

In this example, we use SHA-256 to hash the provided password and compare it with the stored hash in the database. If they match, the user is authenticated.

Authorization

Once a user is authenticated, it's crucial to implement authorization to control access to different parts of the application. Authorization can be role-based or permission-based. Role-based authorization assigns users to specific roles (e.g., "Admin," "User") and defines what actions each role can perform. Permission-based authorization, on the other hand, grants permissions directly to users or roles for fine-grained control.

Here's an example of role-based authorization using VB.NET:

```vbnet
Public Class AuthorizationManager
    Public Function IsUserInRole(username As String, roleName As String) As Boolean
        ' In a real application, you would fetch the user's roles from a database.
        Dim userRoles As List(Of String) = GetRolesForUser(username)

        ' Check if the user is in the specified role.
        Return userRoles.Contains(roleName)
    End Function

    ' Implement a method to retrieve user roles from the database.
    Private Function GetRolesForUser(username As String) As List(Of String)
        ' Retrieve the roles for the given username from the database.
        ' In a real application, this would involve a database query.
        ' Return a list of roles associated with the user.
        Return New List(Of String) From {"User", "Admin"}
    End Function
End Class
```

In this role-based authorization example, we check if a user is in a specific role before allowing access to certain features or resources.

Implementing both authentication and authorization is crucial to building secure VB.NET applications. Depending on your application's requirements, you may also explore more advanced security mechanisms such as OAuth, OpenID Connect, or token-based authentication for web applications. Security should always be a top priority in software development to protect user data and prevent unauthorized access.

Section 15.2: Data Encryption and Security Measures

Data encryption is a crucial aspect of security in VB.NET applications. It ensures that sensitive information, such as passwords or personal data, is protected from unauthorized access. In this section, we'll explore the basics of data encryption and various security measures you can implement in your VB.NET applications.

Data Encryption

Data encryption is the process of converting plaintext data into ciphertext, making it unreadable without the appropriate decryption key. There are various encryption algorithms available in .NET that you can use to secure your data. One commonly used encryption algorithm is the Advanced Encryption Standard (AES).

Here's a simple example of how to encrypt and decrypt data using AES encryption in VB.NET:

```
Imports System.Security.Cryptography
Imports System.Text

Public Class EncryptionManager
    Private Shared key As String = "ThisIsASecretKey12345"
    Private Shared iv As String = "1234567890123456"

    Public Function EncryptData(plainText As String) As String
        Using aesAlg As New AesCryptoServiceProvider()
            aesAlg.Key = Encoding.UTF8.GetBytes(key)
            aesAlg.IV = Encoding.UTF8.GetBytes(iv)

            Dim encryptor As ICryptoTransform = aesAlg.CreateEncryptor(aesAlg
.Key, aesAlg.IV)
            Using msEncrypt As New MemoryStream()
                Using csEncrypt As New CryptoStream(msEncrypt, encryptor, Cry
ptoStreamMode.Write)
                    Using swEncrypt As New StreamWriter(csEncrypt)
                        swEncrypt.Write(plainText)
                    End Using
                End Using
                Return Convert.ToBase64String(msEncrypt.ToArray())
            End Using
        End Using
    End Function

    Public Function DecryptData(cipherText As String) As String
        Using aesAlg As New AesCryptoServiceProvider()
            aesAlg.Key = Encoding.UTF8.GetBytes(key)
            aesAlg.IV = Encoding.UTF8.GetBytes(iv)
```

```
            Dim decryptor As ICryptoTransform = aesAlg.CreateDecryptor(aesAlg
.Key, aesAlg.IV)
            Using msDecrypt As New MemoryStream(Convert.FromBase64String(ciph
erText))
                Using csDecrypt As New CryptoStream(msDecrypt, decryptor, Cry
ptoStreamMode.Read)
                    Using srDecrypt As New StreamReader(csDecrypt)
                        Return srDecrypt.ReadToEnd()
                    End Using
                End Using
            End Using
        End Using
    End Function
End Class
```

In this example, we use AES encryption to encrypt and decrypt data. It's important to keep the encryption key (key) and initialization vector (iv) secure, as they are essential for decryption. In practice, you should store these securely, such as in environment variables or using a key management service.

Other Security Measures

In addition to data encryption, there are several other security measures you should consider for your VB.NET applications:

1. **Secure Password Storage:** Always hash and salt user passwords before storing them in a database. Use strong hashing algorithms like bcrypt or Argon2.

2. **Input Validation:** Validate user inputs to prevent SQL injection, cross-site scripting (XSS), and other injection attacks.

3. **Session Management:** Implement secure session management to prevent session hijacking and fixation.

4. **Cross-Site Request Forgery (CSRF) Protection:** Use anti-CSRF tokens to protect against CSRF attacks.

5. **Security Headers:** Implement security headers like Content Security Policy (CSP) and HTTP Strict Transport Security (HSTS) in your web applications.

6. **Logging and Monitoring:** Implement logging and monitoring to detect and respond to security incidents.

7. **Regular Updates:** Keep your VB.NET framework, libraries, and dependencies up to date to patch security vulnerabilities.

By following these security best practices and staying informed about emerging security threats, you can build robust and secure VB.NET applications that protect user data and maintain the trust of your users.

Section 15.3: Web Security Best Practices

Web security is paramount in VB.NET applications that interact with the internet or handle user data. In this section, we'll explore some of the best practices for securing web applications built with VB.NET.

1. Input Validation

One of the most common attack vectors is improper input handling. Always validate and sanitize user inputs to prevent SQL injection, cross-site scripting (XSS), and other injection attacks. Use input validation libraries or built-in .NET features to filter and validate user inputs effectively.

2. Authentication and Authorization

Implement robust authentication and authorization mechanisms to control access to sensitive areas of your application. Use ASP.NET's built-in Identity framework or other authentication libraries to handle user authentication securely.

3. HTTPS Usage

Always use HTTPS to encrypt data transmitted between the client and the server. Configure your web server to enforce HTTPS, and use tools like Let's Encrypt to obtain free SSL/TLS certificates.

4. Cross-Site Request Forgery (CSRF) Protection

Protect your application against CSRF attacks by implementing anti-CSRF tokens. These tokens validate that requests originate from your application and not from malicious sources.

```
' In your HTML form, include the anti-CSRF token.
<input type="hidden" name="csrfToken" value="<%= AntiForgery.GetTokens() %>">
```

5. Content Security Policy (CSP)

Implement a Content Security Policy (CSP) to restrict the sources from which content can be loaded on your web pages. CSP helps prevent XSS attacks by specifying which domains are allowed to load resources like scripts, styles, and images.

6. HTTP Security Headers

Set security headers in your web application to enhance security. Key security headers include:

- HTTP Strict Transport Security (HSTS): Enforce HTTPS for all requests.
- X-Content-Type-Options: Prevent MIME-type sniffing.
- X-Frame-Options: Control whether your site can be embedded in an iframe.

- X-XSS-Protection: Enable or disable the browser's XSS protection filter.

7. Session Management

Handle session management securely by generating unique session tokens, storing session data securely, and implementing session timeouts. ASP.NET provides built-in support for session management.

8. Error Handling

Be cautious about error messages and stack traces that are visible to end-users. Configure your application to log errors internally while displaying user-friendly error messages.

9. Regular Updates

Keep your VB.NET framework, libraries, and dependencies up to date. Security vulnerabilities can be patched through updates, reducing the risk of exploitation.

10. Security Auditing and Monitoring

Implement security auditing and monitoring to detect and respond to security incidents promptly. Tools like intrusion detection systems (IDS) can help identify unusual activities.

11. Security Testing

Perform regular security testing, including penetration testing and vulnerability scanning, to identify and mitigate potential security issues before they are exploited.

By following these web security best practices, you can significantly enhance the security of your VB.NET web applications and protect sensitive data from various threats. Security should always be a top priority in the development and maintenance of web-based systems.

Section 15.4: Protecting Against Common Attacks

In addition to implementing web security best practices, it's crucial to protect your VB.NET applications against common web application attacks. This section explores some common attack vectors and how to defend against them.

1. SQL Injection (SQLi)

SQL injection attacks occur when an attacker injects malicious SQL queries into input fields or URLs, potentially gaining unauthorized access to your database.

Defense:
- Use parameterized queries or prepared statements to prevent SQL injection.
- Avoid dynamic SQL generation based on user inputs.
- Implement least privilege access to your database to limit potential damage.

```vbnet
' Using parameterized queries in VB.NET
Dim command As New SqlCommand("SELECT * FROM Users WHERE Username = @Username
", connection)
command.Parameters.AddWithValue("@Username", userInput)
```

2. Cross-Site Scripting (XSS)

XSS attacks involve injecting malicious scripts into web pages viewed by other users, allowing attackers to steal session cookies or perform actions on behalf of the user.

Defense:

- Encode user inputs before rendering them in HTML, JavaScript, or other contexts.
- Use the `HttpUtility.HtmlEncode` method in ASP.NET to encode user inputs.

```vbnet
' Encoding user input in ASP.NET
Dim encodedInput As String = HttpUtility.HtmlEncode(userInput)
```

3. Cross-Site Request Forgery (CSRF)

CSRF attacks trick users into performing unintended actions without their knowledge, often through maliciously crafted URLs or forms.

Defense:

- Implement anti-CSRF tokens as mentioned in Section 15.3 to validate requests.
- Ensure that sensitive actions, such as changing passwords or making financial transactions, require additional authentication.

4. Clickjacking

Clickjacking involves tricking users into clicking on a concealed element by overlaying it on top of a legitimate interface.

Defense:

- Use the `X-Frame-Options` HTTP header to prevent your site from being embedded in iframes on other domains.

```vbnet
' Setting X-Frame-Options in ASP.NET
Response.Headers.Add("X-Frame-Options", "DENY")
```

5. Security Misconfigurations

Security misconfigurations, such as leaving debug mode enabled or using default credentials, can expose vulnerabilities in your application.

Defense:

- Regularly review and audit your application's configuration settings.
- Disable unnecessary features, services, and modules.
- Use strong, unique passwords for all accounts and services.

6. Denial of Service (DoS) Attacks

DoS attacks aim to overwhelm your application or server, making it unavailable to legitimate users.

Defense:
- Implement rate limiting and request validation to mitigate DoS attacks.
- Use a Web Application Firewall (WAF) to filter out malicious traffic.

7. Insecure File Uploads

Allowing users to upload files without proper validation can lead to the execution of malicious scripts or the spread of malware.

Defense:
- Only allow specific file types to be uploaded.
- Store uploaded files outside the webroot and serve them through controlled endpoints.

These are just a few of the common attacks your VB.NET applications may face. By understanding these attack vectors and applying the recommended defenses, you can significantly reduce the risk of security breaches and protect your application and its users. Remember that security is an ongoing process, and staying vigilant is essential to keeping your application secure.

Section 15.5: Compliance and Regulatory Considerations

When developing VB.NET applications, it's essential to consider compliance with various regulations and standards, depending on your application's domain and geographic scope. Compliance ensures that your application adheres to legal and industry-specific requirements related to data protection, privacy, and security. This section provides an overview of compliance and regulatory considerations for VB.NET developers.

1. General Data Protection Regulation (GDPR)

If your application processes personal data of European Union (EU) residents, you must comply with GDPR. GDPR imposes strict requirements for data protection and privacy, including user consent, data breach notifications, and the right to be forgotten.

Compliance Steps:
- Implement consent mechanisms for data processing.
- Securely store and process personal data.
- Develop a data breach response plan.
- Provide tools for users to manage their data.

```
' Sample GDPR consent implementation
If userConsentGranted Then
```

```
    ' Process personal data
Else
    ' Limit data processing
End If
```

2. Health Insurance Portability and Accountability Act (HIPAA)

For applications handling healthcare data in the United States, HIPAA compliance is mandatory. HIPAA sets standards for protecting sensitive patient information, including electronic health records (EHRs).

Compliance Steps:

- Ensure data encryption and secure transmission.
- Implement strict access controls to patient data.
- Regularly audit and monitor access logs.
- Develop and test a disaster recovery plan.

```
' Example of access control in VB.NET
If userIsAuthorized Then
    ' Allow access to patient records
Else
    ' Deny access
End If
```

3. Payment Card Industry Data Security Standard (PCI DSS)

If your application handles credit card information, you must adhere to PCI DSS. PCI DSS aims to protect cardholder data and prevent fraud.

Compliance Steps:

- Use secure coding practices to avoid vulnerabilities.
- Encrypt cardholder data during transmission and storage.
- Regularly test and scan for vulnerabilities.
- Restrict access to cardholder data to authorized personnel.

```
' Sample code for encrypting cardholder data
Dim encryptedData As String = EncryptCreditCardData(creditCardNumber)
```

4. Federal Information Security Management Act (FISMA)

Applications used by federal agencies in the United States must comply with FISMA. FISMA requires robust security controls and risk management processes to protect government information systems.

Compliance Steps:

- Implement security controls specified by NIST guidelines.
- Conduct regular security assessments and audits.
- Report security incidents and vulnerabilities to the appropriate authorities.

```
' Example of implementing NIST security controls
ImplementNISTSecurityControls()
```

5. Accessibility Standards (e.g., WCAG)

To ensure your application is accessible to individuals with disabilities, follow accessibility standards like the Web Content Accessibility Guidelines (WCAG). These standards address issues like screen reader compatibility and keyboard navigation.

Compliance Steps:

- Use accessible HTML elements and attributes.
- Provide alternative text for images and multimedia content.
- Ensure keyboard navigation and focus management.

```html
<!-- Sample HTML for providing alternative text -->
<img src="image.jpg" alt="A descriptive alternative text">
```

6. Industry-Specific Regulations

Depending on your application's domain, you may need to comply with industry-specific regulations, such as those in finance, gaming, or energy. Research and understand the relevant regulations for your industry.

Conclusion

Compliance with regulations and standards is crucial to protect your application, users, and data. It helps build trust and credibility with your audience and regulatory authorities. When developing VB.NET applications, always consider the specific compliance requirements that apply to your project and implement the necessary measures to meet those standards.

Chapter 16: Testing and Debugging Strategies

In the software development lifecycle, testing and debugging are crucial phases that ensure the reliability and quality of your VB.NET applications. This chapter explores various strategies, tools, and best practices for effective testing and debugging.

Section 16.1: Unit Testing in VB.NET

Unit testing is a fundamental practice in software development that involves testing individual units or components of your code to verify their correctness. In VB.NET, you can perform unit testing using various frameworks, such as MSTest, NUnit, or xUnit.

Benefits of Unit Testing

1. **Early Bug Detection:** Unit tests help identify bugs and issues early in the development process, reducing the cost of fixing them later.

2. **Regression Testing:** Unit tests serve as regression tests, ensuring that new changes don't break existing functionality.

3. **Improved Code Quality:** Writing unit tests encourages writing modular and maintainable code.

4. **Documentation:** Unit tests can serve as documentation, showcasing how specific functions or methods are expected to behave.

Writing Unit Tests in VB.NET

Here's a basic example of writing unit tests in VB.NET using MSTest:

```
Imports Microsoft.VisualStudio.TestTools.UnitTesting

' The class to be tested
Public Class Calculator
    Public Function Add(a As Integer, b As Integer) As Integer
        Return a + b
    End Function
End Class

' The test class
<TestClass()>
Public Class CalculatorTests
    <TestMethod()>
    Public Sub TestAdd()
        Dim calc As New Calculator()
        Dim result As Integer = calc.Add(2, 3)
        Assert.AreEqual(5, result)
    End Sub
End Class
```

You can run unit tests within Visual Studio or by using command-line tools provided by the testing framework. Running tests should ideally be automated and integrated into your development workflow.

Best Practices for Unit Testing

1. **Isolation:** Ensure that unit tests are isolated from external dependencies, such as databases or web services. Use mocking frameworks when necessary.

2. **Test Coverage:** Aim for high test coverage to verify most of your code's functionality.

3. **Naming Conventions:** Follow a consistent naming convention for your test methods to make them easily discoverable.

4. **Arrange-Act-Assert (AAA):** Structure your tests with a clear arrangement of preconditions, the action being tested, and assertions.

5. **Continuous Integration:** Integrate unit tests into your continuous integration (CI) pipeline to run tests automatically on code commits.

6. **Refactoring:** Refactor and update tests as your code evolves to ensure they remain relevant.

Unit testing is just one aspect of testing in VB.NET. In the following sections of this chapter, we'll explore other testing techniques and debugging strategies to help you build robust and reliable applications.

Section 16.2: Debugging Tools and Techniques

Debugging is an essential skill for developers to identify and resolve issues in their code. In VB.NET, you have access to various debugging tools and techniques that can help streamline this process.

1. Visual Studio Debugger

Visual Studio, the primary integrated development environment (IDE) for VB.NET, offers a powerful debugging toolset. Here are some key features:

- **Breakpoints:** You can set breakpoints in your code to pause execution and inspect variables and the call stack.

- **Watch and Locals Windows:** These windows allow you to view and modify variable values during debugging.

- **Immediate Window:** You can execute code snippets and evaluate expressions interactively in this window.

- **Step Into, Step Over, and Step Out:** These options help you control the flow of execution during debugging.

- **Exception Handling:** Visual Studio provides options to handle exceptions, including breaking on thrown exceptions or only on unhandled exceptions.

2. Console.WriteLine()

A simple yet effective debugging technique is using `Console.WriteLine()` statements to output variable values or messages to the console. This method is particularly useful when debugging console applications.

```
Dim x As Integer = 42
Console.WriteLine($"The value of x is: {x}")
```

3. Logging Frameworks

Using logging frameworks like log4net or Serilog can help you capture and analyze application events and errors. These frameworks allow you to log messages at various levels (e.g., info, warning, error) and configure log output destinations (e.g., files, databases).

```
Imports log4net

' Configure log4net
XmlConfigurator.Configure()

' Create a logger instance
Dim log As ILog = LogManager.GetLogger(GetType(MyClass))

' Log an error message
log.Error("An error occurred: {0}", ex.Message)
```

4. Trace and Debug Classes

The `System.Diagnostics` namespace provides the `Trace` and `Debug` classes for instrumentation and debugging purposes. These classes allow you to trace events and messages, and you can control their output using configuration settings.

```
System.Diagnostics.Trace.WriteLine("This is a trace message.")
System.Diagnostics.Debug.WriteLine("This is a debug message.")
```

5. Third-Party Debugging Tools

Apart from built-in tools, you can also leverage third-party debugging tools like JetBrains' ReSharper or Redgate's .NET Reflector for advanced debugging and code analysis features.

6. Remote Debugging

For scenarios where your application runs on a remote server or device, Visual Studio supports remote debugging. You can attach the debugger to a remote process and debug it as if it were running locally.

Debugging is a skill that improves with practice. It's essential to use a combination of these tools and techniques to diagnose and resolve issues effectively. Additionally, documenting your debugging process can help you and your team understand and fix problems efficiently in the future.

Section 16.3: Code Profiling and Performance Analysis

Optimizing the performance of your VB.NET applications is crucial, especially for software that needs to handle large datasets or high user loads. Code profiling and performance analysis tools can help you identify bottlenecks and areas for improvement in your code.

1. Visual Studio Profiler

Visual Studio provides a built-in profiler that can analyze the performance of your VB.NET application. Here's how you can use it:

- **Instrumentation:** You can choose between sampling and instrumentation profiling methods. Sampling is less intrusive, while instrumentation provides more detailed data.

- **CPU Usage:** The profiler can help you identify which parts of your code consume the most CPU time.

- **Memory Usage:** It can also analyze memory usage, helping you find memory leaks or excessive memory consumption.

- **.NET Object Allocation:** If your application creates a significant number of objects, this profiler can help you optimize object allocation and garbage collection.

2. Benchmarking

Benchmarking involves measuring the performance of specific code sections or functions to identify areas for improvement. You can use the Stopwatch class or benchmarking libraries like BenchmarkDotNet to perform benchmarks.

```
Imports System.Diagnostics

Dim stopwatch As New Stopwatch()
stopwatch.Start()

' Code to benchmark
' ...
```

```
stopwatch.Stop()
Console.WriteLine($"Elapsed Time: {stopwatch.ElapsedMilliseconds} ms")
```

3. Memory Profilers

Memory profilers like JetBrains' dotMemory or Redgate's ANTS Memory Profiler can help you find memory leaks and excessive memory usage in your VB.NET applications. These tools provide insights into object retention and memory usage patterns.

4. Application Profiling

Profiling tools can also analyze application-level performance. They can help you track slow database queries, external service calls, and network latency. Tools like MiniProfiler or Glimpse can be integrated into your web applications for this purpose.

5. ASP.NET Performance Counters

If you're developing ASP.NET applications, you can use performance counters to monitor various aspects of your application's performance. These counters track metrics such as request execution time, request queue length, and memory usage.

6. Database Profiling

For applications heavily reliant on databases, profiling database queries is essential. Tools like Entity Framework Profiler or SQL Server Profiler can help you identify inefficient queries and database performance issues.

7. Load Testing

Load testing tools like Apache JMeter or Microsoft's Visual Studio Load Test can simulate heavy user loads and measure your application's response to stress. This helps you identify how your application performs under various scenarios.

8. Continuous Integration

Consider integrating performance analysis into your continuous integration (CI) pipeline. Tools like SonarQube can automatically analyze code quality and performance metrics as part of your CI process.

Optimizing performance is an iterative process. Profiling and analysis tools can pinpoint performance bottlenecks, but it's essential to use these insights to make targeted improvements. Regular performance testing and monitoring ensure that your VB.NET applications continue to deliver a fast and responsive user experience, even as they evolve and scale.

Section 16.4: Test-Driven Development (TDD)

Test-Driven Development (TDD) is a software development methodology that emphasizes writing tests before writing code. It follows a simple cycle known as the Red-Green-Refactor cycle, where "Red" represents writing a failing test, "Green" means making the test pass by writing code, and "Refactor" is the step to improve the code without changing its behavior. TDD has become increasingly popular as it leads to more robust and maintainable code.

1. Writing Tests

In TDD, you start by writing tests for the functionality you want to implement. These tests should be concise, specific, and focus on a single aspect of your code. For VB.NET, you can use testing frameworks like MSTest, NUnit, or xUnit.

```
Imports Microsoft.VisualStudio.TestTools.UnitTesting

<TestClass>
Public Class MyTests
    <TestMethod>
    Public Sub TestAddition()
        Dim result = MathHelper.Add(2, 3)
        Assert.AreEqual(5, result)
    End Sub
End Class
```

2. Running Tests

After writing a failing test, you run your test suite to verify that the new test indeed fails. This is the "Red" phase of the cycle. You should run your tests frequently, preferably automatically as part of your development workflow.

3. Writing Code

Once you have a failing test, you proceed to write the code that makes the test pass. In the "Green" phase, you write the minimal amount of code necessary to satisfy the test case.

```
Public Class MathHelper
    Public Shared Function Add(a As Integer, b As Integer) As Integer
        Return a + b
    End Function
End Class
```

4. Running Tests Again

After writing the code, you run your test suite again. This time, your goal is to see all tests pass. If any test fails, you need to refine your code until all tests are green.

5. Refactoring

With passing tests, you can confidently refactor your code to improve its design, readability, and performance. You have the safety net of tests to catch any regressions.

6. Repeating the Cycle

TDD is an iterative process. You continue the Red-Green-Refactor cycle for each piece of functionality you develop. This ensures that your codebase remains well-tested and that new code doesn't introduce bugs.

Benefits of TDD

- **Improved Code Quality:** TDD encourages you to write cleaner, modular, and well-structured code.

- **Reduced Debugging:** Catching and fixing issues early in the development process reduces debugging time.

- **Documentation:** Tests serve as living documentation for your codebase, explaining how it should work.

- **Confidence in Changes:** With a comprehensive test suite, you can confidently make changes to your code, knowing that you'll catch regressions.

- **Better Collaboration:** Tests provide a common language between developers and stakeholders, helping clarify requirements.

- **Sustainable Development:** TDD promotes a sustainable pace of development by preventing technical debt and reducing the accumulation of bugs.

While TDD can be challenging to adopt initially, it becomes a valuable practice once you've integrated it into your development workflow. It's particularly useful when working on projects where maintaining code quality and minimizing bugs are critical, such as enterprise-level applications.

Section 16.5: Continuous Integration and Deployment

Continuous Integration (CI) and Continuous Deployment (CD) are practices in software development that aim to improve the quality and delivery speed of software. They involve the automation of various stages of the software development process, from building and testing to deployment. In this section, we'll explore these concepts and their relevance to VB.NET development.

1. Continuous Integration (CI)

Continuous Integration is the practice of frequently integrating code changes into a shared repository, followed by automated build and test processes. The key principles of CI include:

- **Frequent Code Integration:** Developers integrate their code changes into the main repository multiple times a day, ensuring that the codebase remains up-to-date.

- **Automated Builds:** CI systems automatically build the application whenever changes are pushed to the repository. This ensures that the code can be compiled successfully.

- **Automated Testing:** Automated tests, including unit tests and integration tests, are run after each build. If any tests fail, the CI system alerts the team.

- **Immediate Feedback:** Developers receive immediate feedback on the quality of their code changes, allowing them to fix issues quickly.

VB.NET developers can set up CI pipelines using tools like Azure DevOps, Jenkins, or GitHub Actions. These tools allow you to define build configurations, run tests, and trigger builds automatically when code changes are detected.

2. Continuous Deployment (CD)

Continuous Deployment extends CI by automatically deploying code changes to production or staging environments after they pass automated tests. The key principles of CD include:

- **Automated Deployment:** After a successful CI build, the CD pipeline deploys the application to a target environment without manual intervention.

- **Deployment Testing:** CD pipelines often include additional testing in the target environment to ensure that the application functions correctly.

- **Rollback Mechanisms:** CD pipelines should have mechanisms in place to roll back deployments in case issues are detected in the target environment.

- **Environment Parity:** Ensuring that the development, staging, and production environments are as similar as possible helps prevent deployment-related issues.

CD is particularly useful for web applications, APIs, and other systems with frequent updates. It allows teams to release new features and bug fixes quickly and reliably.

3. VB.NET and CI/CD

VB.NET applications can benefit significantly from CI/CD pipelines. These pipelines ensure that your application remains in a deployable state, even as new features and code changes are added. Here's how VB.NET developers can leverage CI/CD:

- **Automated Builds:** Set up CI to automatically build your VB.NET application whenever changes are pushed to the repository. This ensures that your code is always in a compileable state.

- **Automated Testing:** Run unit tests and integration tests as part of your CI pipeline. This helps catch regressions early.

- **Deployment Automation:** Use CD to automate the deployment of your VB.NET application to staging and production environments. Ensure that your deployment process is repeatable and reliable.

- **Configuration Management:** Manage application configurations (e.g., connection strings) separately from the code and ensure that they are injected during deployment.

- **Versioning and Tagging:** Implement versioning and tagging strategies to track which versions of your application are deployed to each environment.

By adopting CI/CD practices, VB.NET development teams can deliver high-quality software more efficiently, reduce manual intervention, and improve collaboration among team members.

In conclusion, Continuous Integration and Continuous Deployment are valuable practices for VB.NET developers looking to streamline their development and delivery processes. These practices help ensure that your VB.NET applications are always in a deployable state and can be released to production with confidence.

Chapter 17: VB.NET Best Practices and Design Patterns

Section 17.1: Coding Standards and Guidelines

Coding standards and guidelines are crucial in any software development project, including VB.NET applications. They ensure consistency, readability, and maintainability of the codebase. In this section, we'll explore the importance of coding standards and provide some best practices for writing clean and maintainable VB.NET code.

Why Coding Standards Matter

1. **Readability:** Well-defined coding standards make your code more readable, not only for you but for other developers who may work on the project. This readability reduces the likelihood of introducing bugs during maintenance.

2. **Consistency:** Consistent code is easier to understand and maintain. It ensures that similar constructs are used consistently throughout the codebase.

3. **Collaboration:** When multiple developers collaborate on a project, coding standards serve as a common set of rules, reducing conflicts and making the code more coherent.

4. **Code Reviews:** Coding standards are valuable during code reviews. Reviewers can focus on logic and architecture instead of pointing out coding style issues.

Here are some best practices for defining and following coding standards in your VB.NET projects:

1. Use a Standard Naming Convention: Choose a consistent naming convention for variables, functions, classes, and namespaces. Common conventions include CamelCase, PascalCase, or underscores between words.

2. Indentation and Formatting: Define rules for code indentation and formatting. For example, specify how to format braces, line breaks, and spacing.

3. Commenting: Encourage meaningful comments in your code to explain complex logic, algorithms, or the purpose of a particular block of code.

4. Consistent File Structure: Define a consistent directory and file structure for your projects. Arrange files logically and consistently to make navigation easier.

5. Error Handling: Establish guidelines for error handling and reporting. Decide when to use Try-Catch blocks and how to handle exceptions gracefully.

6. Code Organization: Encourage the use of regions to organize code into logical sections. However, avoid excessive use of regions, as it can make code harder to read.

7. Code Duplication: Promote the DRY (Don't Repeat Yourself) principle. Avoid duplicating code by creating reusable functions, classes, or libraries.

8. Version Control Practices: Define branching, merging, and commit message conventions when using version control systems like Git.

9. Coding Tooling: Utilize coding tools and IDE extensions that can automatically enforce coding standards, format code, and highlight issues.

10. Code Reviews: Conduct regular code reviews to ensure that coding standards are followed consistently. Use code analysis tools to catch common coding issues.

11. Documentation: Include a coding standards document as part of your project's documentation. This document should detail the coding conventions and guidelines to follow.

12. Continuous Improvement: Coding standards should evolve as your project progresses. Regularly revisit and update them to reflect changing requirements and best practices.

By implementing and following coding standards, you can maintain a high level of code quality, reduce technical debt, and make your VB.NET projects more accessible to other developers. Consistency and readability are key to successful software development, and coding standards are a fundamental part of achieving these goals.

Section 17.2: Design Patterns in VB.NET

Design patterns are proven solutions to common software design problems. They provide a blueprint for solving recurring challenges in a structured and maintainable way. In this section, we'll explore some common design patterns and how they can be applied in VB.NET.

1. Singleton Pattern

The Singleton pattern ensures that a class has only one instance and provides a global point of access to that instance. It's useful for scenarios where you want to control access to resources such as configuration settings or database connections.

```vbnet
Public Class Singleton
    Private Shared _instance As Singleton
    Private Sub New()
    End Sub

    Public Shared Function GetInstance() As Singleton
        If _instance Is Nothing Then
            _instance = New Singleton()
        End If
        Return _instance
    End Function
End Class
```

2. Factory Method Pattern

The Factory Method pattern defines an interface for creating objects but allows subclasses to alter the type of objects that will be created. It's often used in scenarios where the exact class of objects isn't known until runtime.

```vbnet
Public Interface IFactory
    Function CreateProduct() As IProduct
End Interface

Public Class ConcreteFactoryA
    Implements IFactory
    Public Function CreateProduct() As IProduct Implements IFactory.CreatePro
duct
        Return New ConcreteProductA()
    End Function
End Class

Public Class ConcreteFactoryB
    Implements IFactory
    Public Function CreateProduct() As IProduct Implements IFactory.CreatePro
duct
```

```
        Return New ConcreteProductB()
    End Function
End Class
```

3. Observer Pattern

The Observer pattern defines a one-to-many dependency between objects so that when one object changes state, all its dependents are notified and updated automatically. It's commonly used in event-driven systems.

```
Public Interface IObserver
    Sub Update(state As Object)
End Interface

Public Class ConcreteObserver
    Implements IObserver
    Public Sub Update(state As Object) Implements IObserver.Update
        ' Handle the update here
    End Sub
End Class

Public Class Subject
    Private _observers As New List(Of IObserver)
    Private _state As Object

    Public Sub Attach(observer As IObserver)
        _observers.Add(observer)
    End Sub

    Public Sub Detach(observer As IObserver)
        _observers.Remove(observer)
    End Sub

    Public Sub Notify()
        For Each observer In _observers
            observer.Update(_state)
        Next
    End Sub

    Public Property State As Object
        Get
            Return _state
        End Get
        Set(value As Object)
            _state = value
            Notify()
        End Set
    End Property
End Class
```

4. Strategy Pattern

The Strategy pattern defines a family of algorithms, encapsulates each one, and makes them interchangeable. It allows the algorithm to vary independently from clients that use it.

```vb
Public Interface IStrategy
    Sub Execute()
End Interface

Public Class ConcreteStrategyA
    Implements IStrategy
    Public Sub Execute() Implements IStrategy.Execute
        ' Implement strategy A
    End Sub
End Class

Public Class ConcreteStrategyB
    Implements IStrategy
    Public Sub Execute() Implements IStrategy.Execute
        ' Implement strategy B
    End Sub
End Class

Public Class Context
    Private _strategy As IStrategy

    Public Sub New(strategy As IStrategy)
        _strategy = strategy
    End Sub

    Public Sub SetStrategy(strategy As IStrategy)
        _strategy = strategy
    End Sub

    Public Sub ExecuteStrategy()
        _strategy.Execute()
    End Sub
End Class
```

5. Decorator Pattern

The Decorator pattern allows behavior to be added to individual objects, either statically or dynamically, without affecting the behavior of other objects from the same class.

```vb
Public MustInherit Class Component
    Public MustOverride Sub Operation()
End Class

Public Class ConcreteComponent
```

```vb
    Inherits Component
    Public Overrides Sub Operation()
        ' Perform the operation
    End Sub
End Class

Public MustInherit Class Decorator
    Inherits Component
    Protected _component As Component

    Public Sub New(component As Component)
        _component = component
    End Sub

    Public Overrides Sub Operation()
        _component.Operation()
    End Sub
End Class

Public Class ConcreteDecoratorA
    Inherits Decorator
    Public Sub New(component As Component)
        MyBase.New(component)
    End Sub

    Public Overrides Sub Operation()
        ' Add additional behavior before or after the original operation
        MyBase.Operation()
    End Sub
End Class

Public Class ConcreteDecoratorB
    Inherits Decorator
    Public Sub New(component As Component)
        MyBase.New(component)
    End Sub

    Public Overrides Sub Operation()
        ' Add additional behavior before or after the original operation
        MyBase.Operation()
    End Sub
End Class
```

These are just a few examples of

Section 17.3: Refactoring and Code Quality

Refactoring is the process of improving the structure and quality of existing code without changing its external behavior. It's an essential practice in software development that helps maintainability, readability, and extensibility of code. In this section, we'll explore various aspects of refactoring and code quality in VB.NET.

1. Code Smells

Code smells are indicators of potential problems or areas that need improvement in your code. Identifying and addressing code smells can lead to better code quality. Some common code smells include:

- **Long Methods**: Methods that are too long and perform multiple tasks should be divided into smaller, more focused methods for better readability and maintainability.

- **Large Classes**: Classes with too many fields and methods may indicate a lack of cohesion. Consider splitting them into smaller, more specialized classes.

- **Duplication**: Repeated code or logic in multiple places should be extracted into a separate method or class to avoid redundancy.

- **Complex Conditionals**: Nested if statements or complex boolean expressions can be hard to understand. Simplify conditions and use descriptive variable names.

2. Code Refactoring Techniques

Here are some common code refactoring techniques you can apply in VB.NET:

- **Extract Method**: If you have a block of code that performs a specific task, extract it into a separate method with a descriptive name. This improves readability and reusability.

```vbnet
' Before Refactoring
Public Sub CalculateTotal()
    ' Complex logic here
End Sub

' After Refactoring
Public Sub CalculateTotal()
    Dim total = CalculateSubtotal() + CalculateTax()
End Sub

Private Function CalculateSubtotal() As Decimal
    ' Subtotal calculation logic
End Function
```

```
Private Function CalculateTax() As Decimal
    ' Tax calculation logic
End Function
```

- **Rename Variables and Methods**: Use meaningful and descriptive names for variables and methods. This makes it easier for others (and your future self) to understand the code.

```
' Before Refactoring
Dim x As Integer

' After Refactoring
Dim numberOfStudents As Integer
```

- **Remove Dead Code**: Remove unused variables, methods, or imports to declutter your code and reduce confusion.

- **Reduce Method Parameters**: If a method has too many parameters, consider grouping related parameters into a single object or using method chaining.

```
' Before Refactoring
Public Sub ProcessOrder(orderId As Integer, productName As String, quantity A
s Integer, price As Decimal)

' After Refactoring
Public Sub ProcessOrder(order As Order)
```

3. Code Quality Tools

There are several tools available for VB.NET that can help maintain code quality:

- **Static Code Analysis**: Tools like ReSharper and SonarQube can analyze your code for issues, code smells, and potential bugs.

- **Code Metrics**: Visual Studio provides code metrics to measure complexity, maintainability, and other aspects of your code.

- **Unit Testing**: Writing unit tests using a framework like MSTest or NUnit helps ensure that your code behaves as expected and allows for easier refactoring.

- **Continuous Integration**: Tools like Jenkins or Azure DevOps can automate the build and testing process, enforcing code quality checks before code is merged.

- **Code Reviews**: Regular code reviews with peers can help identify code quality issues and provide valuable feedback.

4. Documentation and Comments

Maintaining good documentation and comments is crucial for code quality. Use XML comments to provide information about classes, methods, and parameters. Additionally, document any non-obvious or complex code sections to assist others in understanding your code.

```
''' <summary>
''' Calculates the total price of an order.
''' </summary>
''' <param name="order">The order to calculate.</param>
''' <returns>The total price.</returns>
Public Function CalculateTotal(order As Order) As Decimal
```

In conclusion, refactoring and ensuring code quality are ongoing processes in software development. By following best practices, using refactoring techniques, leveraging code quality tools, and maintaining clear documentation, you can create maintainable, readable, and reliable VB.NET code that stands the test of time.

Section 17.4: Code Reviews and Collaborative Development

Code reviews are an essential part of maintaining code quality and ensuring that a team's collective knowledge and experience are applied to the codebase. In this section, we'll explore the importance of code reviews and how to conduct them effectively in a collaborative development environment using VB.NET.

1. Why Code Reviews Matter

Code reviews offer numerous benefits, including:

- **Bug Detection**: Code reviews can catch bugs and issues early in the development process, reducing the cost and effort required to fix them later.

- **Knowledge Sharing**: Team members can learn from each other's code, share best practices, and gain insights into different approaches and techniques.

- **Consistency**: Code reviews help maintain coding standards and ensure that the codebase adheres to established guidelines.

- **Code Quality**: By reviewing code for readability, maintainability, and efficiency, code reviews contribute to overall code quality.

2. Conducting Code Reviews

Effective code reviews involve a systematic process:

- **Choose the Right Tools**: Utilize code review tools and platforms such as GitHub, GitLab, or Azure DevOps to facilitate the review process.

- **Define Clear Objectives**: Clearly define the goals and expectations of the code review. What aspects of the code should be evaluated (e.g., functionality, readability, performance)?

- **Set a Reviewer and Author**: Assign a reviewer (or multiple reviewers) and the author of the code being reviewed. The reviewer should not be the author to maintain objectivity.

- **Review the Code**: Reviewers should examine the code thoroughly, considering factors like code structure, naming conventions, and error handling. Provide constructive feedback.

- **Automated Checks**: Utilize automated tools for code analysis, style checking, and unit testing to catch issues early.

- **Provide Feedback**: Reviewers should offer specific feedback, pointing out what's done well and suggesting improvements. Avoid personal criticism; focus on the code.

- **Iterate**: The author may need to make changes based on feedback. The code may go through several iterations of review and improvement.

- **Approve and Merge**: Once the code meets the defined criteria and receives approval from the reviewer(s), it can be merged into the codebase.

3. Code Review Checklist

Consider using a code review checklist to ensure thorough and consistent reviews. Here's a sample checklist for VB.NET:

- **Naming Conventions**: Are variable and method names descriptive and follow naming conventions?

- **Code Structure**: Is the code well-structured, with appropriate use of classes, methods, and modules?

- **Error Handling**: Does the code handle exceptions and errors gracefully?

- **Performance**: Are there any potential performance bottlenecks or inefficient algorithms?

- **Code Comments**: Are comments used to explain complex logic or non-obvious decisions?

- **Code Duplication**: Is there any duplicated code that can be refactored into reusable methods?

- **Testing**: Is the code covered by unit tests, and do the tests pass?

- **Security**: Is sensitive data handled securely, and are there measures against common security vulnerabilities?

- **Documentation**: Is the code documented with XML comments where necessary?

- **Consistency**: Does the code adhere to the team's coding standards and conventions?

4. Collaborative Development

Effective code reviews are a part of collaborative development. Encourage collaboration by:

- **Regular Meetings**: Hold regular team meetings to discuss code reviews, share insights, and address challenges.

- **Pair Programming**: Consider pair programming sessions where two developers work together on a task, providing instant feedback.

- **Knowledge Sharing**: Share knowledge through documentation, presentations, and informal discussions.

- **Feedback Culture**: Foster a culture of constructive feedback and continuous improvement within the team.

In conclusion, code reviews are an integral part of collaborative development in VB.NET projects. They enhance code quality, promote knowledge sharing, and help maintain consistency within the codebase. By following best practices for conducting code reviews and embracing a collaborative development culture, development teams can produce higher-quality software.

Section 17.5: Maintaining and Evolving VB.NET Projects

Maintaining and evolving VB.NET projects is a critical aspect of software development. In this section, we'll explore the strategies and best practices for keeping your projects up-to-date, improving them over time, and ensuring their longevity.

1. The Need for Maintenance

Software projects require ongoing maintenance for several reasons:

- **Bug Fixes**: Bugs and issues inevitably arise after deployment, and they need to be addressed promptly.

- **Security Updates**: As new vulnerabilities are discovered, it's crucial to apply security updates to protect your application and user data.

- **Technology Advancements**: Programming languages, frameworks, and libraries evolve. Maintaining your project ensures compatibility with new technologies.

- **User Feedback**: User feedback and changing requirements may lead to feature enhancements or modifications.

Version control systems (e.g., Git) play a vital role in project maintenance. Here's how to use them effectively:

- **Branching**: Create feature branches for new development and bug-fixing branches for addressing issues. Use a branching strategy like GitFlow.

- **Commit Messages**: Write clear and concise commit messages to document changes. Include references to issues or user stories.

- **Pull Requests**: Use pull requests (or merge requests) for code review and discussion before merging changes into the main branch.

- **Documentation**: Maintain up-to-date documentation, including a README file, installation instructions, and user guides.

3. Continuous Integration and Continuous Deployment (CI/CD)

Implementing CI/CD pipelines automates the build, test, and deployment process. Benefits include:

- **Automated Testing**: Run unit tests, integration tests, and code analysis automatically with each code change.

- **Frequent Releases**: CI/CD enables frequent and reliable releases, reducing the risk of introducing defects.

- **Rollback Capability**: Quickly roll back to a previous version if issues arise after deployment.

- **Deployment Strategies**: Implement deployment strategies like blue-green or canary releases for minimal user impact.

4. Code Refactoring

Regular code refactoring is essential for maintaining code quality and readability:

- **Identify Smells**: Look for code smells such as duplicated code, long methods, or complex conditional statements.

- **Refactor Safely**: Refactor small sections at a time, ensuring that unit tests pass after each change.

- **Maintain Coding Standards**: Enforce coding standards during refactoring to maintain consistency.

5. Dependency Management

Manage dependencies carefully to prevent security vulnerabilities and compatibility issues:

- **Dependency Scanning**: Use dependency scanning tools to identify vulnerabilities in third-party libraries.

- **Dependency Updates**: Regularly update dependencies to their latest versions. Automated tools can help with this.

6. Performance Optimization

Monitor and optimize application performance:

- **Profiling**: Use profiling tools to identify performance bottlenecks.

- **Caching**: Implement caching mechanisms to reduce database and network requests.

7. User Feedback and Testing

Engage with users to collect feedback and conduct testing:

- **User Feedback**: Actively seek user feedback to prioritize feature requests and improvements.

- **User Testing**: Conduct usability testing to identify user experience issues.

8. Monitoring and Error Tracking

Implement monitoring and error tracking solutions to proactively identify and resolve issues:

- **Log Aggregation**: Aggregate and centralize logs for easy analysis.

- **Error Tracking**: Use error tracking tools to receive notifications of application errors.

9. Long-Term Planning

Plan for the long-term sustainability of your project:

- **Technology Stack**: Consider the longevity of the technologies you use. Evaluate the need for migrating to newer platforms or languages.

- **Scalability**: Ensure that your application can scale to meet growing user demands.

- **Backups and Disaster Recovery**: Implement backup and disaster recovery plans to protect against data loss.

In conclusion, maintaining and evolving VB.NET projects is an ongoing process that involves version control, documentation, automated testing, code refactoring, dependency management, performance optimization, user feedback, monitoring, and long-term planning. By following these best practices, you can ensure the reliability and sustainability of your VB.NET projects as they evolve over time.

Chapter 18: Building Enterprise-Level Applications

Section 18.1: Scalability and Performance Optimization

Building enterprise-level applications requires careful consideration of scalability and performance. In this section, we'll explore strategies and best practices for designing and optimizing applications to handle high workloads, ensuring they perform efficiently even under heavy traffic.

1. Scalability Fundamentals

Scalability is the ability of an application to handle increased loads without sacrificing performance. It's essential for enterprise-level applications that may experience rapid growth. Consider the following aspects of scalability:

- **Horizontal Scaling**: Add more servers or instances to distribute the load. This approach is often achieved using load balancers.

- **Vertical Scaling**: Increase the resources (CPU, RAM) of a single server. Vertical scaling has limits but can be effective for certain workloads.

- **Stateless Architecture**: Design applications to be stateless, where each request is independent. This simplifies horizontal scaling.

2. Database Scalability

Database scalability is a critical consideration for enterprise applications. Here's how to approach it:

- **Replication**: Use database replication for read-heavy workloads. Replicated databases can distribute read queries across multiple servers.

- **Sharding**: Implement database sharding to partition data across multiple database servers. This is effective for write-heavy applications.

- **Caching**: Utilize caching mechanisms to reduce the load on the database. Popular caching solutions include Redis and Memcached.

3. Content Delivery Networks (CDNs)

CDNs are networks of distributed servers that cache and deliver content closer to end-users. They are valuable for improving the performance and availability of web applications:

- **Static Asset Caching**: Store static assets (images, CSS, JavaScript) in CDNs to reduce the load on your servers and decrease latency.

- **Global Content Distribution**: CDNs have servers worldwide, reducing the distance data must travel and improving page load times for users.

4. Load Balancing

Load balancing distributes incoming traffic across multiple servers to ensure optimal resource utilization and prevent overload:

- **Load Balancer Types**: Choose between hardware and software load balancers. Software load balancers are often more flexible and cost-effective.
- **Health Checks**: Implement health checks to ensure that only healthy servers receive traffic.

5. Asynchronous Processing

Offload time-consuming tasks to asynchronous processes or background workers:

- **Message Queues**: Use message queues (e.g., RabbitMQ, Apache Kafka) to decouple components and process tasks asynchronously.
- **Batch Processing**: Consider batch processing for tasks that can be delayed, such as generating reports.

6. Performance Optimization

Efficient code and resource utilization are essential for performance:

- **Code Profiling**: Use profiling tools to identify performance bottlenecks in your code.
- **Caching**: Implement data and query caching to reduce the load on databases and external services.
- **Content Compression**: Compress responses to reduce bandwidth usage and improve load times.

7. Scalability Testing

Regularly test your application's scalability to identify weaknesses and plan for growth:

- **Load Testing**: Simulate high loads to determine how your application behaves under stress.
- **Stress Testing**: Exceed the application's expected limits to identify potential bottlenecks.

8. Failover and Redundancy

Plan for failover and redundancy to ensure high availability:

- **Failover Strategies**: Implement strategies for automatic failover to backup servers or data centers in case of hardware or software failures.

- **Data Backup**: Regularly back up data to prevent data loss in case of failures.

9. Monitoring and Alerting

Continuous monitoring and alerting help you proactively address issues:

- **Real-time Monitoring**: Use monitoring tools to track the health and performance of your application and infrastructure.

- **Alerting**: Set up alerts to notify your team of performance degradation or system failures.

In conclusion, building enterprise-level applications that can scale and perform well under heavy loads requires careful planning and the adoption of various strategies. Scalability, database optimization, CDN usage, load balancing, asynchronous processing, performance optimization, scalability testing, failover planning, and monitoring are all essential aspects of building robust and high-performing enterprise applications.

Section 18.2: Distributed Systems and Microservices

In the world of enterprise-level applications, distributed systems and microservices architecture have gained significant popularity. They offer a way to design scalable, maintainable, and fault-tolerant applications. In this section, we will delve into the concepts of distributed systems and microservices and how they can benefit your enterprise-level projects.

1. Distributed Systems

A distributed system is a collection of interconnected, autonomous computers that work together to achieve a common goal. Key characteristics of distributed systems include:

- **Decentralization**: Distributed systems consist of multiple nodes, often geographically dispersed, that operate independently but collaborate to provide a unified service.

- **Scalability**: Distributed systems can scale horizontally by adding more nodes to handle increasing loads.

- **Fault Tolerance**: They are designed to withstand hardware failures or network issues without a complete service interruption.

- **Data Consistency**: Ensuring data consistency across distributed nodes is a significant challenge. Techniques like distributed databases and consensus algorithms (e.g., Paxos, Raft) are used.

2. Microservices Architecture

Microservices architecture is an approach to building software as a collection of small, independent services, each responsible for a specific business capability. Key principles of microservices include:

- **Service Decoupling**: Microservices are loosely coupled, meaning they can be developed, deployed, and scaled independently. This fosters agility.

- **Single Responsibility**: Each microservice focuses on a specific function, following the Single Responsibility Principle (SRP).

- **APIs and Communication**: Microservices communicate via APIs (typically RESTful or gRPC), allowing them to work together to fulfill complex requests.

- **Polyglot Persistence**: Microservices can use different data storage technologies (polyglot persistence) based on their specific needs.

3. Benefits of Microservices

Microservices offer several advantages for enterprise-level applications:

- **Scalability**: Each microservice can be scaled independently, allowing you to allocate resources where needed.

- **Faster Development**: Smaller, focused teams can work on individual microservices, speeding up development cycles.

- **Isolation**: A failure in one microservice doesn't necessarily impact the entire system.

- **Technology Diversity**: Choose the best technology stack for each microservice's requirements.

- **Ease of Maintenance**: Smaller codebases are easier to maintain and update.

4. Challenges of Microservices

While microservices have many benefits, they also introduce challenges:

- **Complexity**: Managing a large number of microservices can become complex. Proper orchestration and monitoring are essential.

- **Data Consistency**: Maintaining data consistency in a distributed environment can be challenging.

- **Deployment and DevOps**: Microservices require efficient deployment pipelines and DevOps practices.

- **Testing**: End-to-end testing of microservices can be complex and resource-intensive.

Microservices are well-suited for various use cases:

- **E-commerce Platforms**: Handling product catalogs, user authentication, order processing, and recommendation engines as separate microservices.

- **Financial Systems**: Managing accounts, transactions, payments, and fraud detection as microservices.

- **Social Media**: User profiles, news feeds, notifications, and messaging can each be separate microservices.

- **IoT and Real-Time Systems**: Processing data from sensors, managing devices, and providing real-time analytics through microservices.

In conclusion, distributed systems and microservices are powerful architectural approaches for building scalable and maintainable enterprise-level applications. While they offer numerous benefits, it's essential to carefully plan and manage the complexities they introduce. The choice between traditional monolithic architecture and microservices should be based on your project's specific requirements and goals.

Section 18.3: Enterprise Integration Patterns

Enterprise integration patterns (EIPs) are a set of design patterns used to solve common integration challenges in enterprise-level applications. They provide a systematic way to address issues related to communication, data transformation, and process orchestration when integrating various systems and services within an organization. In this section, we will explore some fundamental EIPs and how they can enhance the integration capabilities of your software.

1. Message Channel

A message channel is a communication channel that enables the exchange of messages between different parts of a system. It acts as an intermediary for sending and receiving messages, allowing components to communicate asynchronously. Message channels can be implemented using various technologies such as message queues, publish-subscribe systems, or simple in-memory buffers.

Example: In a microservices architecture, message channels can be used to decouple services. When a service generates an event or message, it can publish it to a message channel, and other services can subscribe to that channel to receive and process the message.

2. Message Router

Message routers are responsible for directing messages from a source to one or more destinations based on predefined criteria. They make decisions about where a message should be delivered, often using content-based routing or routing tables. Message routers are essential for ensuring that messages are delivered to the appropriate components within a system.

Example: In an e-commerce platform, a message router can direct incoming orders to different processing modules based on the customer's location. Orders from customers in Europe might be routed to a data center in Europe, while orders from North America are directed to a different data center.

3. Message Translator

Message translation is a common requirement when integrating systems that use different data formats or protocols. A message translator, also known as a data mapper, is responsible for converting messages from one format or protocol to another, ensuring that systems can communicate effectively.

Example: When integrating a legacy system that uses XML messages with a modern system that expects JSON, a message translator can be used to convert XML messages into JSON format before delivery.

4. Content Enricher

A content enricher is used to enhance a message's content by adding additional information or context to it. This enrichment process typically involves fetching data from external sources or databases and incorporating it into the original message. Content enrichment is valuable when integrating systems that rely on supplementary data.

Example: In a supply chain management system, a content enricher can add real-time weather data to a shipment tracking message, providing valuable information about weather conditions during transportation.

5. Message Filter

Message filters are used to evaluate messages against predefined criteria and determine whether they should be allowed to proceed in the integration process. Filters can be applied to messages based on their content, properties, or other attributes.

Example: In a financial application, a message filter can be used to screen incoming transactions for potential fraud. Transactions that meet specific criteria, such as unusual activity or high-value transfers, may trigger further investigation.

6. Aggregator

Aggregators combine multiple related messages into a single message. This is particularly useful when dealing with messages that are split into smaller parts during transmission and need to be reassembled.

Example: In a large-scale e-commerce system, customer orders might be split into separate messages for processing. An aggregator can be used to combine these individual order items into a complete order before further processing or fulfillment.

7. Scatter-Gather

The scatter-gather pattern involves sending a message to multiple recipients and collecting their responses. This pattern is valuable when you need to obtain various responses to a single request and make decisions based on the collected results.

Example: In a travel booking system, a search request for available flights can be scattered to multiple airline services. The responses from different airlines are then gathered and presented to the user for comparison.

Enterprise integration patterns provide a powerful toolbox for designing and implementing effective integration solutions in complex enterprise environments. By understanding and applying these patterns, software architects and developers can streamline communication between systems, reduce integration challenges, and create more robust and flexible applications. When building enterprise-level applications, it's crucial to choose the appropriate EIPs that align with your integration requirements and system architecture.

Section 18.4: Workflow and Business Process Automation

Workflow and business process automation are critical components of enterprise-level applications, helping organizations streamline operations, improve efficiency, and reduce errors. In this section, we will explore the concepts of workflow management and automation, including their benefits, common use cases, and best practices.

1. Understanding Workflow

A workflow represents a series of interconnected steps or tasks that need to be executed to achieve a specific business goal. Workflows can range from simple linear sequences of tasks to complex, branching processes involving multiple stakeholders and decisions. Workflow management involves designing, modeling, executing, and monitoring these sequences of tasks to ensure they are carried out efficiently and accurately.

Benefits of Workflow Management: - Efficiency: Workflows automate repetitive tasks, reducing manual effort and minimizing errors. - **Visibility**: Organizations gain visibility into the status of ongoing processes, allowing for better decision-making. - **Consistency**: Standardized workflows ensure that processes are executed consistently, adhering to established best practices. - **Compliance**: Workflows can enforce compliance with regulatory requirements by embedding them into processes. - **Scalability**: Workflow automation scales easily to accommodate growing workloads and changing business needs.

2. Workflow Automation Technologies

Workflow automation can be implemented using various technologies and tools, including dedicated workflow engines, business process management (BPM) platforms, and low-code/no-code development platforms. These technologies provide features for designing, orchestrating, and monitoring workflows.

Example Code (Using a Hypothetical Workflow Engine):

```
// Define a workflow for processing customer orders
var workflow = new Workflow("OrderProcessingWorkflow");

// Define workflow steps
var receiveOrder = new ReceiveOrderStep();
var validateOrder = new ValidateOrderStep();
var prepareItems = new PrepareItemsStep();
var shipOrder = new ShipOrderStep();

// Connect workflow steps
workflow.ConnectSteps(receiveOrder, validateOrder);
workflow.ConnectSteps(validateOrder, prepareItems);
workflow.ConnectSteps(prepareItems, shipOrder);

// Execute the workflow for a specific order
var order = new Order();
workflow.Execute(order);
```

3. Common Use Cases

Workflow and business process automation are used in various industries and scenarios. Some common use cases include: - **Document Approval**: Automating the approval of documents, such as purchase orders, invoices, and contracts. - **Employee Onboarding**: Guiding new employees through the onboarding process, from paperwork to training. - **Inventory Management**: Automating stock replenishment, order fulfillment, and inventory tracking. - **Customer Support**: Managing and tracking customer support tickets from creation to resolution. - **Loan Approval**: Automating the loan application and approval process in financial institutions. - **Healthcare Workflows**: Managing patient admissions, treatment plans, and billing processes in healthcare.

4. Best Practices

When implementing workflow and business process automation, consider the following best practices: - **Process Analysis**: Carefully analyze existing processes before automation to identify bottlenecks and areas for improvement. - **User Involvement**: Involve end-users in the design and testing of automated workflows to ensure they meet real-world needs. - **Integration**: Ensure that automated workflows can integrate with existing systems and data sources. - **Monitoring and Analytics**: Implement monitoring and analytics tools to track workflow performance and identify optimization opportunities. - **Scalability**: Design workflows to scale with business growth by using modular and adaptable components. -

Security and Compliance: Implement security measures to protect sensitive data and ensure compliance with industry regulations. - **Testing and Validation**: Thoroughly test automated workflows to identify and resolve potential issues.

Workflow and business process automation play a pivotal role in modern enterprise software development. They empower organizations to streamline operations, improve productivity, and enhance the overall customer and employee experience. By adopting best practices and leveraging automation technologies, businesses can achieve greater efficiency and agility in their daily operations.

Section 18.5: Enterprise Application Security

Enterprise application security is a paramount concern in today's digital landscape. As organizations increasingly rely on software systems for their critical operations, safeguarding these applications from security threats and vulnerabilities is essential. In this section, we will explore the key aspects of enterprise application security, including best practices and strategies for protecting valuable assets.

1. The Importance of Application Security

Enterprise applications often store and process sensitive data, making them attractive targets for cyberattacks. A security breach can result in data theft, financial losses, damage to reputation, and legal consequences. Therefore, a comprehensive approach to application security is crucial.

Example Scenario: Imagine an e-commerce platform that handles customer payment information. If this system's security is compromised, it could lead to unauthorized access to credit card details and financial fraud.

2. Key Principles of Application Security

To ensure the security of enterprise applications, several fundamental principles should be followed:

2.1. Authentication and Authorization

Implement strong authentication mechanisms to verify users' identities and grant access only to authorized individuals. Role-based access control (RBAC) and permissions management are essential for restricting access to sensitive resources.

```java
// Example code in a Java Spring Security configuration
@Override
protected void configure(HttpSecurity http) throws Exception {
    http
        .authorizeRequests()
            .antMatchers("/admin/**").hasRole("ADMIN")
            .antMatchers("/user/**").hasAnyRole("ADMIN", "
```

Chapter 19: VB.NET in the IoT and Embedded Systems

Section 19.1: Internet of Things (IoT) Overview

The Internet of Things (IoT) is a transformative technology that connects everyday objects and devices to the internet, allowing them to collect and exchange data. This section provides an overview of IoT, its significance, and its applications in various domains.

1. What Is the Internet of Things (IoT)?

IoT refers to the network of physical objects, devices, vehicles, buildings, and other items embedded with sensors, software, and connectivity to collect and exchange data over the internet. These "smart" objects can interact with each other, users, and their environments, creating a vast ecosystem of interconnected devices.

Example: A smart thermostat that adjusts temperature based on user preferences and weather conditions is an IoT device.

2. Significance of IoT

IoT has gained immense importance due to its potential to revolutionize multiple industries:

2.1. Improved Efficiency

IoT can enhance operational efficiency by automating tasks, monitoring equipment, and optimizing processes. This efficiency translates to cost savings and increased productivity.

Example Scenario: Sensors in manufacturing machines can detect faults and trigger maintenance, minimizing downtime.

2.2. Data-Driven Insights

The data generated by IoT devices can provide valuable insights for decision-making. Real-time data analytics and predictive maintenance are among the benefits.

Example: Smart agriculture uses IoT to monitor soil conditions and weather, optimizing crop yields.

2.3. Enhanced User Experience

IoT can improve user experiences through personalized services and automation. Smart homes and wearable devices are prime examples.

Example: A fitness tracker monitors a user's activity and offers personalized health recommendations.

2.4. Safety and Security

IoT can enhance safety by monitoring environments for hazards and security by providing surveillance and access control.

Example Scenario: IoT-based security cameras send alerts if unusual activity is detected.

3. IoT Applications

IoT finds applications in diverse sectors, including:

- **Smart Cities**: IoT is used for traffic management, waste collection, and energy conservation.
- **Healthcare**: Wearable devices and remote monitoring improve patient care.
- **Manufacturing**: IoT optimizes production processes and quality control.
- **Transportation**: IoT enables real-time tracking and maintenance of vehicles.
- **Agriculture**: Smart farming uses IoT for precision agriculture.
- **Retail**: IoT enhances inventory management and customer experiences.
- **Energy**: Smart grids and meters optimize energy distribution.

4. IoT Challenges and Considerations

While IoT offers numerous benefits, it also poses challenges:

4.1. Security Concerns

The large number of connected devices increases the attack surface, making security a top priority. Devices must be protected from unauthorized access and data breaches.

4.2. Privacy Issues

IoT devices collect vast amounts of data, raising privacy concerns. Regulations like GDPR address data protection.

4.3. Interoperability

Ensuring that IoT devices from different manufacturers can work together seamlessly is essential for widespread adoption.

4.4. Scalability

IoT deployments must scale to accommodate growing numbers of devices and data volume.

4.5. Data Management

Efficiently storing, processing, and analyzing the massive amounts of data generated by IoT devices is a significant challenge.

5. Conclusion

IoT is reshaping industries and daily life, offering unprecedented opportunities and challenges. Understanding the fundamentals of IoT and its applications is essential for developers and organizations looking to leverage this technology for innovation and efficiency. In the following sections, we will delve deeper into developing IoT applications using VB.NET.

Section 19.2: Developing IoT Applications

In Section 19.1, we explored the fundamentals of the Internet of Things (IoT). Now, we'll dive into the practical aspects of developing IoT applications using VB.NET. Developing for IoT involves creating software that interacts with physical devices, collects data from sensors, and makes intelligent decisions based on that data. Here are the key steps involved in developing IoT applications:

1. Hardware Selection

Selecting the right hardware is crucial for your IoT project. This includes choosing microcontrollers or development boards, sensors, actuators, and communication modules that suit your application. Popular choices for IoT hardware include Arduino, Raspberry Pi, and ESP8266/ESP32.

2. Sensor Integration

IoT applications often rely on sensors to collect data from the physical world. Sensors can measure temperature, humidity, light, motion, and more. Integrating sensors with your hardware and writing code to read data from them is an essential step.

```
' VB.NET code to read data from a temperature sensor (example)
Dim sensorPin As Integer = 2 ' GPIO pin connected to the sensor
Dim temperature As Double

' Initialize the sensor
Dim sensor As New TemperatureSensor(sensorPin)

' Read temperature data
temperature = sensor.ReadTemperature()
```

3. Data Processing

IoT applications process the data collected from sensors to make informed decisions. This may involve data filtering, aggregation, and analysis. VB.NET provides libraries and tools for efficient data processing.

```
' VB.NET code for data processing (example)
Dim data As List(Of Double) = GetSensorData() ' Get sensor data
Dim averageTemperature As Double = data.Average()
```

4. Connectivity

IoT devices need a way to communicate with other devices or the cloud. This can be achieved through various communication protocols such as Wi-Fi, Bluetooth, Zigbee, or cellular networks. VB.NET supports network communication, making it possible to send data to remote servers or receive commands.

```
' VB.NET code for sending data over Wi-Fi (example)
Dim wifiModule As New WiFiModule()
wifiModule.Connect("SSID", "Password")

' Send data to a remote server
Dim dataToSend As String = "Sensor data"
wifiModule.SendData(dataToSend)
```

5. Cloud Integration

IoT applications often leverage cloud services for data storage, processing, and remote control. Services like Azure IoT Hub, AWS IoT Core, and Google Cloud IoT provide platforms for managing IoT devices and data. Integrating your VB.NET application with these platforms enables cloud-based IoT solutions.

```
' VB.NET code for sending data to Azure IoT Hub (example)
Dim azureIoTHub As New AzureIoTHub("DeviceConnectionString")
azureIoTHub.SendTelemetryData(dataToSend)
```

6. Security

Security is paramount in IoT applications to protect data and devices from unauthorized access and cyber threats. Implementing authentication, encryption, and access control measures is essential.

7. Power Management

Efficient power management is crucial for battery-operated IoT devices. Writing code that minimizes power consumption and manages sleep modes is important for extending battery life.

8. User Interface

If your IoT application requires a user interface, you can create one using VB.NET's Windows Forms or other graphical libraries. This allows users to interact with the IoT device or monitor its status.

9. Testing and Deployment

Thoroughly test your IoT application on real hardware to ensure it functions correctly. Once tested, deploy the application to your IoT devices, whether they are located in homes, industrial settings, or other environments.

Developing IoT applications with VB.NET combines the power of a versatile programming language with the hardware capabilities of IoT devices. It enables developers to create innovative solutions that bridge the physical and digital worlds, making IoT technology accessible to a wide range of applications and industries.

Section 19.3: Embedded Systems and Microcontrollers

In this section, we delve into the world of embedded systems and microcontrollers in the context of IoT development. Embedded systems are specialized computing systems designed to perform specific tasks, and microcontrollers are the heart of these systems. We will explore the role of microcontrollers in IoT applications, their programming, and key considerations when working with them.

1. Understanding Microcontrollers

A microcontroller is a compact integrated circuit (IC) that contains a processor core, memory, input/output peripherals, and often, communication interfaces. Microcontrollers are designed for low-power and real-time applications, making them ideal for IoT devices. They come in various architectures, such as ARM, AVR, and PIC, each with its own set of features and capabilities.

2. Microcontroller Programming

Programming microcontrollers involves writing code to control the behavior of the device. Low-level languages like C and assembly are commonly used for microcontroller programming due to their efficiency and direct hardware access. VB.NET is not typically used for microcontroller programming, but it can be employed for higher-level tasks in an IoT system.

```
' VB.NET code for high-level IoT control (example)
Dim sensorData As Double
Dim threshold As Double = 25.0

' Read sensor data
sensorData = ReadSensor()

' Check if data exceeds threshold
If sensorData > threshold Then
    ' Take action, e.g., send an alert
    SendAlert("Sensor data exceeds threshold!")
End If
```

3. Interfacing with Microcontrollers

To interface with microcontrollers in an IoT system, you often need to develop firmware that runs on the microcontroller itself. This firmware can be written in C or assembly language. The firmware communicates with sensors, actuators, and other hardware components, making decisions based on the data it collects.

4. Real-Time Requirements

Many IoT applications demand real-time responsiveness, especially in scenarios where immediate action is necessary. Microcontrollers are well-suited for real-time tasks, thanks to their deterministic execution and low-latency characteristics.

5. Power Management

IoT devices often run on battery power, so efficient power management is crucial. Microcontrollers are designed for low-power operation and offer sleep modes that conserve energy when the device is idle.

6. Sensor Integration

Microcontrollers are the bridge between sensors and IoT applications. They collect data from sensors, process it, and transmit relevant information to other parts of the IoT system. Integrating sensors with microcontrollers may involve protocols like I2C, SPI, or UART.

7. Communication Interfaces

Microcontrollers support various communication interfaces such as UART, SPI, I2C, and GPIO pins. These interfaces allow microcontrollers to connect with other devices, including sensors, actuators, and communication modules.

8. IoT Protocols

Microcontrollers can communicate with the cloud or other IoT devices using protocols like MQTT, CoAP, or HTTP. Implementing these protocols in microcontroller firmware is crucial for IoT device connectivity.

9. Developing Firmware

Writing firmware for microcontrollers requires expertise in low-level programming. If you're new to microcontroller development, it's advisable to start with development boards like Arduino or Raspberry Pi, which offer a simplified programming environment.

10. Debugging and Testing

Debugging embedded systems can be challenging, but tools like in-circuit debuggers (ICDs) and serial communication can help diagnose issues. Rigorous testing of the firmware on real hardware is essential to ensure reliable operation.

Microcontrollers are the backbone of IoT devices, providing the computing power necessary to collect data, make decisions, and control the physical world. Understanding how to program and work with microcontrollers is a fundamental skill for IoT developers, allowing them to create efficient, responsive, and low-power solutions for a wide range of applications.

Section 19.4: Real-Time Processing with VB.NET

Real-time processing is a critical aspect of many IoT and embedded systems applications. It involves handling data and events as they occur, often with strict timing constraints. In this section, we explore how VB.NET can be used to implement real-time processing in IoT and embedded systems, even though it may not be the primary language for such tasks.

1. Understanding Real-Time Processing

Real-time processing refers to the ability to respond to events or input data within a predictable and guaranteed time frame. In IoT and embedded systems, real-time capabilities are essential for applications like industrial automation, robotics, and sensor data acquisition.

2. Real-Time Constraints

Real-time systems have various levels of constraints, such as hard real-time, where a missed deadline can lead to catastrophic consequences, and soft real-time, where some flexibility in meeting deadlines is acceptable. The choice of real-time constraints depends on the specific application requirements.

3. Challenges with VB.NET for Real-Time

VB.NET is primarily a high-level, garbage-collected language, which can introduce non-deterministic behavior and latency in real-time systems. However, you can still use VB.NET for real-time processing if the timing requirements are not extremely strict or if you employ workarounds.

4. VB.NET Multithreading

VB.NET supports multithreading, which can help improve real-time responsiveness by parallelizing tasks. By carefully managing threads and priorities, you can mitigate some of the non-determinism associated with garbage collection.

```vbnet
' VB.NET code demonstrating multithreading
Dim thread1 As New Thread(AddressOf RealTimeTask1)
Dim thread2 As New Thread(AddressOf RealTimeTask2)

' Set thread priorities
thread1.Priority = ThreadPriority.Highest
thread2.Priority = ThreadPriority.Highest

' Start the threads
thread1.Start()
thread2.Start()
```

5. Reducing Non-Deterministic Behavior

To minimize non-deterministic behavior in VB.NET, consider using real-time extensions or external libraries designed for real-time systems. These extensions can provide more precise control over timing and resource management.

6. Real-Time Operating Systems (RTOS)

For applications with stringent real-time requirements, using a real-time operating system (RTOS) is often the best approach. RTOSs provide deterministic scheduling and resource management, allowing you to achieve precise timing in your IoT and embedded systems.

7. Hardware Acceleration

In some cases, you may need to offload real-time tasks to specialized hardware, such as digital signal processors (DSPs) or field-programmable gate arrays (FPGAs). These hardware accelerators can perform computations with low latency, freeing up the main processor for other tasks.

8. Testing and Validation

Real-time systems require rigorous testing and validation to ensure they meet their timing constraints. Use tools like schedulability analysis and simulation to verify that your system can meet its real-time requirements.

9. Choosing the Right Approach

When implementing real-time processing in VB.NET, carefully assess your application's timing requirements and constraints. For soft real-time applications, VB.NET with multithreading and optimization may suffice. For hard real-time applications, consider using an RTOS or hardware acceleration.

In conclusion, while VB.NET may not be the first choice for real-time systems, it can still be used effectively with careful consideration of its limitations and the application's specific requirements. Real-time processing is crucial in many IoT and embedded systems scenarios, and choosing the right approach is essential for success.

Section 19.5: IoT Security and Challenges

IoT (Internet of Things) devices are becoming increasingly prevalent in various domains, from smart homes to industrial automation. However, with this proliferation of connected devices comes a growing concern for security. In this section, we delve into IoT security considerations and the challenges associated with securing IoT ecosystems.

1. The Importance of IoT Security

Security is paramount in IoT systems because these devices often handle sensitive data and perform critical functions. Inadequate security can lead to data breaches, device manipulation, and even safety hazards.

2. IoT Security Challenges

2.1. Resource Constraints

Many IoT devices have limited computing power and memory, making it challenging to implement robust security measures. Lightweight cryptography and efficient algorithms are essential in such environments.

2.2. Network Vulnerabilities

IoT devices frequently communicate over wireless networks, which can be susceptible to eavesdropping, jamming, and Man-in-the-Middle (MitM) attacks. Encryption, secure communication protocols, and network monitoring are critical defenses.

2.3. Device Authentication

Ensuring that only authorized devices can interact with an IoT network is crucial. Techniques like mutual authentication and secure bootstrapping are used to establish trust between devices and the network.

2.4. Firmware and Software Updates

Keeping IoT device firmware up-to-date is essential to patch security vulnerabilities. However, delivering updates to resource-constrained devices without disrupting their operations can be challenging.

3. Security Best Practices

3.1. Secure Boot and Trusted Execution Environments (TEEs)

Implement secure boot processes to ensure that only authentic and unaltered firmware is loaded. TEEs, such as ARM TrustZone, provide isolated execution environments for secure operations.

3.2. Data Encryption

Encrypt data both at rest and in transit. Modern cryptographic libraries designed for IoT, like mbed TLS, offer lightweight encryption solutions suitable for resource-constrained devices.

3.3. Access Control and Authorization

Enforce strict access control policies and implement role-based authorization. Limit the privileges of each IoT device to the minimum necessary for its function.

3.4. Continuous Monitoring

Implement real-time monitoring of network traffic and device behavior. Anomalies and suspicious activities should trigger alerts for rapid response.

3.5. Over-the-Air (OTA) Updates

Develop a secure OTA update mechanism that verifies the integrity of updates before installation. Digital signatures and secure channels for updates are vital.

4. IoT Security Standards and Frameworks

Several organizations, such as NIST and IoT Security Foundation, have published guidelines and frameworks for securing IoT systems. Adhering to these standards can help ensure a higher level of security.

5. Security by Design

Security should be integrated into the design and development of IoT devices from the outset. Threat modeling, risk assessments, and security testing should be part of the development lifecycle.

6. User Education

End-users of IoT devices should also be educated about security best practices, including setting strong passwords, configuring firewalls, and recognizing phishing attempts.

7. Future Challenges

As IoT technology evolves, new security challenges will emerge. Quantum computing, 5G networks, and the increasing complexity of IoT ecosystems will require continuous adaptation and innovation in IoT security.

In conclusion, IoT security is a complex and evolving field that demands careful attention. The benefits of IoT can only be fully realized when the associated security risks are adequately addressed. As IoT continues to expand, the development and implementation of robust security measures will be crucial to safeguarding connected devices and the data they handle.

Chapter 20: The Future of VB.NET Development

Section 20.1: VB.NET in Modern Software Development

Visual Basic .NET (VB.NET) has a rich history and has played a significant role in software development for many years. As technology evolves, VB.NET continues to be relevant in modern software development, and in this section, we'll explore its place in the ever-changing landscape.

1. A Language with Legacy

VB.NET, an evolution of the classic Visual Basic language, maintains backward compatibility, making it easy for developers with a VB6 background to transition to modern development. Organizations with legacy VB.NET codebases find it cost-effective to maintain and enhance their applications.

2. .NET Core and .NET 5+

With the release of .NET Core and the subsequent transition to .NET 5 and beyond, VB.NET is part of the broader .NET ecosystem. This allows VB.NET developers to leverage the benefits of cross-platform development, performance improvements, and modern language features.

3. Web Development with ASP.NET Core

VB.NET can be used to build web applications using ASP.NET Core. While C# is the more commonly used language for web development in this stack, VB.NET remains a viable choice, especially for organizations that have a VB.NET talent pool.

4. Desktop Applications with .NET Core and WinForms

Developers can create cross-platform desktop applications using VB.NET, .NET Core, and WinForms. This combination provides a way to build modern, responsive desktop apps that work on Windows, macOS, and Linux.

5. Open Source Contributions

The .NET community values open source contributions. Developers proficient in VB.NET can actively participate in open source projects, expanding their skills and contributing to the broader developer community.

6. Modernization Efforts

Organizations with legacy VB6 applications are investing in modernization efforts to migrate to VB.NET. This ensures continued support, security, and compatibility with modern platforms.

7. Emerging Technologies

VB.NET can be used to develop applications for emerging technologies such as Internet of Things (IoT), cloud computing, and mobile development. Its adaptability makes it suitable for a wide range of projects.

8. The VB.NET Community

The VB.NET community remains active and supportive. Developers can find resources, forums, and user groups dedicated to VB.NET, facilitating knowledge sharing and problem-solving.

9. Future Adaptations

Microsoft has shown commitment to VB.NET by including it in the .NET 5+ ecosystem. While its adoption may not be as widespread as C#, VB.NET remains a choice for developers and organizations looking for a familiar and productive development environment.

In conclusion, VB.NET continues to have a place in modern software development. Its legacy, compatibility, and adaptability make it a valuable choice for various projects. Whether you're maintaining legacy systems, modernizing applications, or exploring new technologies, VB.NET remains a language with a future in the diverse landscape of software development.

Section 20.2: Emerging Technologies and Trends

In the rapidly evolving field of software development, staying up-to-date with emerging technologies and trends is crucial. As VB.NET developers, it's essential to be aware of the directions in which the industry is moving. Let's explore some of the prominent emerging technologies and trends that may impact VB.NET development.

1. .NET 6 and Beyond

Microsoft's commitment to .NET is unwavering, with regular updates and improvements. VB.NET developers should keep an eye on the latest .NET releases, such as .NET 6 and upcoming versions. These updates bring new language features, performance enhancements, and cross-platform capabilities that can benefit VB.NET projects.

2. Blazor for Web Development

Blazor, a web framework by Microsoft, allows developers to build web applications using C# and VB.NET. It offers both server-side and client-side options, making it a versatile choice for web development. VB.NET developers can leverage Blazor for modern web application development.

3. Artificial Intelligence (AI) and Machine Learning (ML)

AI and ML are transforming various industries. VB.NET developers interested in AI can explore libraries and frameworks like ML.NET, a cross-platform, open-source machine learning framework that integrates seamlessly with VB.NET applications.

4. Cloud-Native Development

Cloud-native development focuses on building applications optimized for cloud environments. VB.NET developers can adapt by learning about containerization technologies like Docker and Kubernetes and exploring cloud providers like Azure, AWS, and Google Cloud.

5. Serverless Computing

Serverless computing simplifies infrastructure management, allowing developers to focus on code. VB.NET developers can build serverless applications using Azure Functions or AWS Lambda, enabling efficient, scalable, and cost-effective solutions.

6. DevOps and CI/CD

DevOps practices and continuous integration/continuous deployment (CI/CD) pipelines have become essential in modern software development. Learning how to implement CI/CD for VB.NET projects can improve development efficiency and code quality.

7. Internet of Things (IoT)

IoT is a growing field with applications in smart devices, healthcare, and more. VB.NET developers can explore IoT development by using platforms like Azure IoT or Raspberry Pi with Windows 10 IoT Core.

8. Cross-Platform Development

Cross-platform development tools like Xamarin enable VB.NET developers to create mobile applications for iOS and Android using a single codebase. This approach saves time and resources for mobile app development.

9. Progressive Web Apps (PWAs)

PWAs offer a responsive and native app-like experience on the web. VB.NET developers can leverage technologies like Blazor and Service Workers to create PWAs that work seamlessly across different devices and browsers.

10. Cybersecurity

As cyber threats continue to evolve, cybersecurity remains a critical concern. VB.NET developers should be well-versed in security best practices to protect applications and data from potential threats.

11. Quantum Computing

While still in its infancy, quantum computing holds the promise of solving complex problems that are currently infeasible for classical computers. Developers with a curiosity for cutting-edge technology may explore quantum computing in the future.

In summary, VB.NET developers can embrace emerging technologies and trends to stay relevant and competitive in the ever-evolving software development landscape. Continuous learning and adaptability are key to harnessing the potential of these technologies and driving innovation in VB.NET development.

Section 20.3: Community and Open Source Contributions

Community engagement and open source contributions play a pivotal role in the growth and evolution of any programming language or framework, including VB.NET. In this section, we'll explore the significance of community involvement and how VB.NET developers can contribute to open source projects.

1. Community Support and Collaboration

VB.NET has a dedicated community of developers who actively engage in discussions, provide assistance on forums, and share their knowledge and experiences. Engaging with this community is valuable for learning, troubleshooting, and collaborating on projects.

2. Stack Overflow and Forums

Platforms like Stack Overflow host discussions related to VB.NET, where developers can seek solutions to specific issues, share their expertise, and contribute by answering questions. Active participation on these platforms helps build a strong developer network.

3. GitHub and Open Source

GitHub is a hub for open source projects, and many VB.NET libraries and tools are hosted there. Developers can explore existing projects, report issues, and submit pull requests to contribute enhancements or bug fixes. Contributing to open source projects is an excellent way to gain experience and give back to the community.

```
' Example of contributing to an open source project on GitHub
Public Class MyFeature
    Public Shared Function Add(a As Integer, b As Integer) As Integer
        Return a + b
    End Function
End Class
```

4. Creating VB.NET Libraries

Developers can create their own VB.NET libraries and share them with the community. This contributes to the ecosystem and can be a valuable resource for others. Hosting projects on platforms like NuGet allows easy distribution.

5. Organizing Meetups and Webinars

Organizing local or online meetups and webinars focused on VB.NET can foster knowledge sharing and networking among developers. These events provide opportunities to learn from experts and connect with peers.

6. Writing Documentation and Tutorials

Creating documentation and tutorials for VB.NET libraries or frameworks can help others understand and use them effectively. Well-documented projects are more likely to gain adoption and contribute to the community's learning.

7. Mentoring and Teaching

Experienced VB.NET developers can mentor newcomers or teach programming courses. Sharing knowledge and guidance with others can accelerate the learning process and strengthen the community.

8. Advocating for VB.NET

Advocacy for VB.NET is essential to maintain its relevance. Developers can advocate for VB.NET in their organizations, promote its benefits, and contribute to discussions about its future.

9. Feedback to Microsoft

Providing feedback to Microsoft about VB.NET, its features, and improvements is valuable. Participating in the language design process, if possible, helps shape the language's future.

10. Promoting Inclusivity and Diversity

Ensuring that the VB.NET community is inclusive and welcoming to developers of all backgrounds is crucial. Encouraging diversity and respectful interactions contributes to a healthier and more vibrant community.

In conclusion, community and open source contributions are essential for the growth and sustainability of VB.NET. By actively participating in the community, sharing knowledge, and contributing to open source projects, VB.NET developers can both advance their own skills and contribute to the broader programming community.

Section 20.4: Preparing for the Next Generation of VB.NET

The world of software development is dynamic and ever-evolving, and VB.NET is no exception. In this section, we'll discuss how developers can prepare for the future of VB.NET by staying up-to-date with industry trends, embracing modern practices, and ensuring their skills remain relevant.

1. Embracing .NET 6 and Beyond

With the release of .NET 6, Microsoft has introduced significant updates and improvements to the .NET ecosystem. Developers should keep abreast of these changes and consider migrating their VB.NET applications to the latest versions of the .NET framework for enhanced performance, security, and features.

2. Learning New Language Features

Although VB.NET remains a valuable language, it's essential to explore new language features and paradigms introduced in the latest .NET versions. Familiarize yourself with modern practices such as C# 9.0 records, pattern matching, and nullable reference types, which can enhance your programming skills.

```csharp
// Example of C# 9.0 record
public record Person(string FirstName, string LastName);

// Example of pattern matching
if (obj is string str && str.Length > 10)
{
    Console.WriteLine($"String '{str}' has more than 10 characters.");
}
```

3. Leveraging Cross-Platform Development

Developers should consider cross-platform development to reach a broader audience. Technologies like Blazor allow you to build web applications that run on both the web and desktop. Exploring Xamarin for mobile app development is another way to expand your skill set.

4. Embracing DevOps and CI/CD

Implementing DevOps practices and continuous integration/continuous deployment (CI/CD) pipelines can streamline software development and deployment processes. Automation, testing, and rapid releases are critical in modern development workflows.

5. Exploring Cloud and Microservices

Understanding cloud computing platforms such as Microsoft Azure, Amazon Web Services (AWS), and Google Cloud Platform (GCP) is essential. Microservices architecture, containerization with Docker, and orchestration with Kubernetes are also valuable skills for scalable and maintainable applications.

6. Evolving Security Practices

As security threats continue to evolve, developers should stay updated on security best practices. Implementing encryption, authentication, and authorization measures is crucial to protect data and applications.

7. Fostering Collaboration and Soft Skills

Soft skills, such as communication, teamwork, and problem-solving, are increasingly important in software development. Collaborate effectively with cross-functional teams and stakeholders to deliver successful projects.

8. Preparing for AI and Machine Learning Integration

AI and machine learning are transforming various industries. Consider how these technologies can enhance your applications and be prepared to integrate them where relevant.

9. Lifelong Learning

In the rapidly changing world of technology, learning never stops. Invest time in continuous learning, whether through online courses, workshops, or reading industry publications. Networking with other developers and attending conferences can also provide valuable insights.

10. Adaptability and Resilience

Lastly, adaptability and resilience are essential traits for developers. Embrace change, learn from failures, and be open to new challenges. These qualities will serve you well in navigating the evolving landscape of VB.NET and software development.

In summary, the future of VB.NET development is promising for those who are willing to adapt, learn, and embrace modern practices. By staying informed about industry trends, upgrading skills, and maintaining an open mindset, developers can position themselves for success in the ever-changing world of software development.

Section 20.5: Continual Learning and Advancement

In the fast-paced world of software development, continual learning and professional advancement are paramount. This final section emphasizes the importance of staying committed to personal growth and keeping abreast of industry developments.

1. Stay Updated with Emerging Technologies

Technology evolves rapidly, and new programming languages, frameworks, and tools emerge regularly. Keep a watchful eye on emerging technologies that align with your interests and career goals. Platforms like GitHub, Stack Overflow, and programming communities can be valuable sources of information.

2. Open Source Contributions

Contributing to open-source projects is an excellent way to enhance your skills, collaborate with other developers, and give back to the community. Many successful developers have started by contributing to open source.

3. Mentorship and Knowledge Sharing

As you gain experience, consider becoming a mentor to junior developers. Sharing your knowledge not only helps others but also reinforces your own understanding of concepts.

4. Networking

Networking is fundamental in the tech industry. Attend conferences, meetups, and online events to connect with professionals, exchange ideas, and discover job opportunities. LinkedIn and other social media platforms can also facilitate networking.

5. Certifications and Advanced Degrees

Obtaining certifications or pursuing advanced degrees, such as a Master's in Computer Science or relevant fields, can open up new career paths and enhance your expertise. Certifications like AWS Certified Solutions Architect or Google Professional Cloud Architect are recognized in the cloud computing industry.

6. Soft Skills Development

Technical skills are vital, but soft skills are equally important. Effective communication, teamwork, problem-solving, and adaptability are traits that employers highly value. Invest in honing these skills to excel in your career.

7. Specialization

Consider specializing in a specific domain or technology area. Whether it's cybersecurity, data science, artificial intelligence, or web development, specialization can make you a sought-after expert in your chosen field.

8. Entrepreneurship

For those with an entrepreneurial spirit, venturing into startups or building your own software products can be an exciting path. Entrepreneurship offers the opportunity to apply your skills to create solutions for real-world problems.

9. Contribute to the Community

Active involvement in the developer community, such as organizing meetups or workshops, writing technical blogs, or hosting webinars, not only benefits others but also enhances your visibility and credibility.

10. Work-Life Balance

Remember the importance of work-life balance. Burnout is a real concern in the tech industry due to the demands of the job. Prioritize your well-being and mental health to ensure a sustainable and fulfilling career.

11. Reflect and Set Goals

Periodically reflect on your career progress and set new goals. Whether it's mastering a new programming language, leading a project, or taking on a leadership role, having clear objectives can guide your career trajectory.

In conclusion, the world of software development is a journey of lifelong learning and advancement. Embrace change, stay curious, and remain adaptable. The skills you've acquired throughout this book on VB.NET will serve as a strong foundation for your career, but it's your commitment to continual growth and development that will truly set you apart and lead to a fulfilling and successful career in the dynamic field of software development.